GIRLS' LIFE MAGAZINE

GL Bye Bye Boredom!
The Girls' Life
BIG Book of Fun

Written by Lisa Mulcahy

Edited by Karen Bokram, Sarah Cordi, and Kelly White

Illustrated by Frank Montagna

Scholastic Inc.
New York • Toronto • London • Auckland • Sydney
Mexico City • New Delhi • Hong Kong • Buenos Aires

ISBN 0-439-44976-6

Copyright © 2003 by Girls' Life Magazine

Design: Mark Neston
All rights reserved. Published by Scholastic Inc.

SCHOLASTIC and associated logos are trademarks
and/or registered trademarks of Scholastic Inc.

12 11 10 9 8 7 6 5 4   4 5 6 7 8/0

Printed in the U.S.A.

First Scholastic printing, March 2003

Contents

Hey You!

What are you doing? If you're thinking, "A whole lotta nada," it's officially time to start doing a whole lotta *something*! Clearly, you're a clever and resourceful gal—after all, you've got your hands on *Bye Bye Boredom! The Girls' Life Big Book of Fun*. This is the first and most crucial step to bidding boring days buh-bye!

It's a big, bright, fun, and exciting world out there (and in your backyard and in your room), so get up and get going! With *Bye Bye Boredom!* you'll never be stumped for something to do, play, create, whip up, invent, try, or ponder. Consider this book your official boredom buster!

For each to-do, we've tipped you off as to whether you can swing it when you're hanging solo, or if you're better off with a bud or an entire posse of pals to up the fun factor. You'll also find a list of supplies you'll need. You won't have to break your piggy bank or sleuth out some impossible-to-find specialty shop for anything. Nope. We're talking on-the-spot, on-the-cheap, instant FUN! Almost everything you need should be at your fingertips or simple enough to find or borrow. Some supplies aren't even supplies, really—like a great view of the horizon, or a yard dusted in leaves, or a vivid imagination.

Whether you're aspiring to add amusement to a sunny Saturday or just want to warm up a snowy day, *Bye Bye Boredom!* is for you. So...what in the name of BIG ideas are you waiting for!? You've got tons to do!

Karen

Karen Bokram
Editor-in-Chief, *GL*

Chapter 1

You, You, You!

Hanging solo? So, your best bud is tied up with family stuff, and the rest of your crew are nowhere to be found. Even your sibs are off doing their own things. You're so bored, you'd find watching paint dry fascinating. But wait! Why be bored when the most interesting person on earth is right in your room—YOU!

The Name Game

What You'll Need:

✳ **A BOOK OF BABY NAMES** (IF MOM DOESN'T HAVE ONE LYING AROUND, ASK A BUD WITH A YOUNGER SIBLING) **OR, GO ONLINE!**

Do you know what your name means? If not, it's a snap to find out! Flip through a book of baby names, or go online and type your name into a search engine like YAHOO! or GOOGLE. Plenty of websites are dedicated to everything about names—meanings, language, country of origin, nicknames, spelling variations, and other trivial tidbits about your tag.

Though it's a piece of cake to do detective work on your first and middle names, it can be tough to uncover info on less-than-common last names. But check out a database of last names, corresponding coats of arms, and family crests at www.last-names.net.

BONUS IDEA: Get the scoop on your friends' names, and fill them in on your discoveries. At your next get-together, check out the goods on each other's names. Of course, you can't resist doing a little...um...background check on the names of all the cuties in your class, too. Bet you didn't know that Brian means, "The Strong One." For a real hoot, uncover name-related personality traits! Go to *Namely-Yours* at http://www.namely-yours.com and type in your crush's name. Plus, it's the perfect way for you and your buds to give your crushes secret code names. Dish out loud on the daily doings of "The Strong One" without being found out!

Check out the top 10 most popular girls' names in the United States recently. Go online and find where your name fell on the list in the year you were born.

EMILY: *COMES FROM AMELIA, MEANING "INDUSTRIOUS"*

HANNAH: *"GRACEFUL"*

MADISON: *"CHILD OF MAUDE"*

SAMANTHA: *"LISTENER" OR "FLOWER"*

ASHLEY: *"FROM THE ASH GROVE"*

SARAH: *"PRINCESS"*

ELIZABETH: *"CONSECRATED TO GOD"*

KAYLA: *"CROWN OF LAUREL"*

ALEXIS: *"THE PROTECTOR AND HELPER OF MANKIND"*

ABIGAIL: *"FATHER'S JOY"*

Picture This: Draw Your Self-Portrait

What You'll Need:

* ❋ A SKETCH PAD OR DRAWING PAPER
* ❋ DRAWING PENCILS
* ❋ ERASER
* ❋ A MIRROR OR A FAVORITE PHOTO OF YOURSELF
* ❋ GLUE, SCISSORS, MAGAZINES, AND COLORED PAPER
  (IF YOU GO FOR THE EXTRA IDEA, BELOW)

Use a mirror or picture of yourself to capture your glorious, glamorous essence! Before you begin drawing, take a good look at yourself. What do you see—eyes, nose, mouth, of course. But anything else? Do you see shadows on your face? Do certain areas appear lighter and other areas darker, like your cheekbones? If you really look at your face, you will see different variations of shade, depending on where light is hitting you. Even if you don't necessarily notice them, capturing shadows is exactly what brings any drawing to life. Sometimes, it's tricky to start drawing— especially a self-portrait! But, just jump right in. When sketching, your lines don't have to be perfectly straight—it's a free form of drawing. Arm yourself with an eraser, but refrain from using it too much. Don't worry about making yourself look exactly like you do in real life or in a photo. If you're concerned about proportions, like that you'll sketch your nose way too high, or draw extremely crooked lips, don't be—this takes major practice. So be patient!

Basic Guidelines:

1. After you've taken a good look at yourself, sketch your face as a circle, oval, or square, depending on its shape.

2. Divide the oval into fourths by drawing a "cross." What you do is very lightly draw a straight vertical line down the center, and then a straight horizontal line through the middle of the oval.

3. Now it's time to draw your eyes. Look into the mirror or at your photo again. Draw an eye on each side of the vertical line (and slightly above the horizontal line, depending on how far your eyes are set from the center of your face).

4. Sketch your nose. Generally speaking, noses are centered about where the horizontal and vertical lines intersect. Use your pencil again to approximate size, and lightly sketch the shape of your nose.

5. Sketch your mouth. Look into the mirror or at your photo again, and approximate the distance of your mouth from your nose. Mark the length and width and center of your lips, and then lightly sketch them.

6. Trace over your light sketches to make them more pronounced, and add details like hair, eyebrows, eyelashes, freckles, or moles.

7. Add shadows accordingly, paying attention to the lightest areas (perhaps the whites of your eyes) and the darkest places (maybe the centers of your eyes or nostrils), and shade everything else based on those extremes.

8. If you can still see guidelines, erase them or shade over where necessary. You should now have a spitting image of yours truly!

Journal the Day Away

SOLO

What You'll Need:
 ✳ YOUR JOURNAL
 ✳ YOUR FAVORITE PEN (OR COMPUTER FOR EVEN SPEEDIER JOURNALING!)
 ✳ A COMFY SPOT TO WRITE IN

If you love expressing your deepest thoughts in your journal, there's no better cure for the what-to-do blues than to write about everything you're thinking. The point of a journal is to write whatever you want, however you want to write it. That's called free-writing. It's totally, absolutely for you and you alone.

If you're just starting a journal, remember that anything, and everything, goes—poetry, observations, working out your probs on paper, just keeping a log of what's up on any particular day. Your journal can be funny, serious, filled with long entries, stuffed with short sentences—it can be anything you want it to be.

Make Keepable Resolutions

SOLO

What You'll Need:
 ✳ PEN AND PAPER
 ✳ WILLPOWER

It doesn't have to be the New Year to make a change. Don't put off making resolutions or setting goals until the next January 1st rolls around. Absolutely any day is a great day to set goals. Like, how about today?

Just be reasonable and realistic about it. Making a resolution like, "Tomorrow is officially the last day I will eat sugared cereal for breakfast. I will never touch it again. Instead, I will get up early and exercise before school," is not exactly realistic. While completely admirable, it's just way too much to take on at once.

Try setting your sights on just one goal at a time: "I'll eat corn muffins instead of sugared cereal, at least during the week." If you set lofty goals that require way too much change all at once, you'll overwhelm yourself and get frustrated. Frustration can lead to feeling disappointed and exhausted, and possibly bailing on the whole thing.

So, when it comes to setting goals, it's majorly important that you don't bite off more than you can chew!

THE GL GUIDE TO GOAL-GETTING:

1. *Start Drafting:* For optimal success, don't let a million "I will" and "I won't" thoughts buzz around in your head. Write down what you'd like to accomplish. When you know what you want, goal-getting is much easier.

2. *Prioritize:* If you have a list of several goals, decide which one to go after first. Like, should you work on raising your math grade so you don't see a "D" come report card time? Or, resolve to stop biting your nails? Not a stumper—go for the grades!

3. *Be Strategic:* Once you decide which goal to start on, determine how you plan to make a goal turn into reality. Make a list of ways to raise your grade. Ask for extra help after class, make flash-cards, study with a friend, plan for tests and quizzes several nights before, ask Mom or Dad about a tutor....

4. *Take Baby Steps:* Don't decide that, as of tomorrow, you will never *ever* eat another bowl of sugared cereal as long as you live. Go at it day by day. Start by cutting back. If you now eat cereal seven days a week, try eating it four days a week for two weeks. Then, three days a week for two weeks, and then only two days a week, etc. Once you've quelled the cereal beast, add in the morning jumping jacks and pushup routine.

5. *Cut Yourself Some Slack:* Mapping out your goals doesn't mean everything is set in stone. Allow room for flexibility. As you set out on the road to resolutions, you'll discover what steps are working, what steps need tweaking and what isn't working at all. Change your plan accordingly. If you want to keep a chart or journal to track your successes, that's a great idea! Go slowly, and allow yourself a slip-up here or there.

BONUS: Your self-esteem will soar. Promise!

Cool and Collected: Start a Collection

What You'll Need:

✳ **Passion, interest, and commitment!**

Hello Kitty…postcards…antique dolls…stuffed animals…vintage purses…angel figurines…you name it, you can collect it. Collecting is an ongoing hobby—and for some, it's a way of life. The most dedicated collectors might spend their entire lives collecting something like salt-and-pepper shakers. They might have hundreds and hundreds of S&P shakers from all over the world, and yet they're always looking for more! But no need to make a lifetime commitment or put an addition onto your house in order to have some fun collecting. Most likely, you already have several collections. In some collecting circles, three of anything is considered a collection.

Collect anything from posters to teacups to foreign coins, and everything in between. If you love black cats, become a black cat collecting connoisseur! Once you fall in love with your collection, your friends and family will always be on the look-out for black cat goodies for you. It's really fun to buy presents for someone with a passion for collecting (you know your gift will be a hit)! Another cool thing about collecting is that you can start your collection at any age, and keep it going for as long as you like!

Over time, your collection will likely become more focused. You might realize that little ceramic cats are your favorites—so, you can narrow your search and set out to find only ceramic kitties. Collecting something really specific is more fun because it becomes a challenge to track down exactly what you want. Finding the perfect little china cat somewhere totally unexpected is what makes collecting such a rush.

Also, make sure your collection doesn't swallow your living space. Set aside a shelf on your bookcase, or find a wall-mounted shelf on the cheap. You want your collection safely out of the way, yet on display for admiring. Happy hunting!

Do Something Sweet for Someone

What You'll Need:

✳ **ABSOLUTELY NOTHING BUT WONDERFUL YOU**

Isn't it awesome when someone does something super-sweet for you outta-the-blue? Ever rushed from your house leaving your room a total pig sty only to return home to find it spotless? Not only did Mom toss all those empty soda cans, but she also changed your sheets and washed your dirty clothes!

What about the time you were totally stressed and your BFF showed up on your doorstep? She sweetly convinced you to abandon your science project for 20 minutes, so you two could take a stress-free stroll around the neighborhood. Once you took in some fresh air, you felt a zillion times better.

We all have a million things going on, but it's great to remember what matters most—friends and family. You don't have to throw a huge birthday bash for a bud or buy your BFF a super-expensive designer purse to brighten her day—a genuine smile or a thoughtful note does the trick.

Additional Ideas:

❀ Wash the dinner dishes (without being asked).

❀ Instead of camping out by the front door and rummaging through the grocery bags for some Lucky Charms, help Mom bring in the groceries and put them away (without being asked).

❀ Set up a study-buddy session for your bud who's struggling in science (without being asked).

❀ Take your camera out with you, and snap some great photos of your friends. Get doubles made, and give your pals pictures of themselves with the whole gang.

❀ Offer to baby-sit for your siblings, nephew, or cousin, for free!

Put Together Your Photo Album

What You'll Need:
* ❇ YOUR PHOTO ALBUM
* ❇ THOSE BOXES OF SNAPSHOTS YOU'VE BEEN MEANING TO ORGANIZE

Finish what you started! Make today the day you complete work on the photo album you began months ago.

First, page through your album to refresh your memory and review your picture assortment. Did you group photos together in any special way—like putting all your family photos on the same page or in the same general section? If you like a particular picture arrangement, keep it, and add more pictures in the same way. If not, remove the pictures and start again.

You can make labels for your photos, accent your album pages with artwork, add poetry—you name it! Spending an afternoon arranging your favorite memories is a fun way to spend the day.

Introduce Yourself to Three Potential Friends

SOLO
(BUT YOU'RE MAKING NEW FRIENDS)

What You'll Need:
* ❇ A FRIENDLY SMILE
* ❇ AN OUTGOING ATTITUDE

Make a promise to yourself right now to stop breezing past the girl at the next locker. Swear that tomorrow you'll say "hi, " and strike up some small talk about school, after-school activities, the lunch menu, or whatever. It takes a little nerve, but forget the sweat and just be friendly. Promise to introduce yourself to someone else the *next* day, and the day after that, too! Within less than a week, you will have met three potential friends and be well on your way to expanding your social circle. And, as an added benefit, your self-esteem will totally get a boost!

Meditate

What You'll Need:

❋ **A QUIET SPOT AND ABOUT A HALF HOUR**

Turn down the noise in your mind by meditating. All you have to do is close your eyes, breathe deeply, and think of nothing in particular. This form of deep relaxation will reward you with a totally refreshed perspective.

Sign Here: Start an Autograph Collection

SOLO OR WITH A BUD

What You'll Need:

❋ **AN AUTOGRAPH BOOK (OR PAPER) AND A PEN**
❋ **INTERNET ACCESS**
❋ **AN OCCASIONAL TRIP OUTTA THE HOUSE**

Try collecting celebrities...or, rather, their signatures! Like other collections, getting your paws on autographs takes dedicated detective work.

How to Sleuth Out Sigs:

❀ Keep a pen and paper (or better yet, your autograph book) with you at all times—you never know when you might see a star.

❀ Peruse your local paper for upcoming events. Attend college and professional sporting events, celebrity ice-skating shows, plays and concerts. Some celebs (especially up-and-comers) set aside time to sign autographs before or after concerts. Just be prepared to stand in line!

❀ Check out the classifieds in movie magazines, like *Premiere*, for ads offering autographs or autographed pics for sale.

❀ Comb thrift stores, flea markets, and hobby shows for autographed pics, too!

❀ Type "autograph" into an Internet search engine, and you'll find sites covering every aspect of autograph collecting.

The Best Things in Life Are Free: So Volunteer Your Time

SOLO

What You'll Need:
* ❋ COMPASSION

Read Dr. Seuss's *Green Eggs and Ham* to a gang of 4-year-olds at the library. Sign up for an Adopt-a-Grandparent program at a nursing home. Walk pups at the pound. Be a junior candy-striper. Lending your hand, and your heart, to others rules, no matter how you do it.

Be a Lifesaver: Get Certified

SOLO, WITH A BFF, OR A FAMILY MEMBER

What You'll Need:
* ❋ A FIRST AID CLASS

Everybody should know lifesaving techniques, like cardiopulmonary resuscitation (CPR), to revive someone who has stopped breathing— and the Heimlich maneuver, to rescue a person from choking. To learn, you need to sign up for a class with an experienced instructor. Get in touch with the Red Cross for a referral to a first aid class in your area.

Also, encourage your buds and relatives to join with you. Remember, there is safety in numbers—the more people certified in first aid, the safer the world will be! The Red Cross is also a great place to get certified if you're planning to baby-sit. You'll be trained to handle a variety of emergency situations, and you'll be confident in your ability to be the very best sitter.

Talk to a Geranium

Just for Fun

For years, scientific research has told us that talking to plants actually helps them grow. So ask your mom's daffodils or white orchids *whassup*! No need to worry, unless they answer you back!

Speak-Up: Improve Your Speaking Voice

What You'll Need:

❋ A BLANK AUDIOTAPE

❋ A TAPE RECORDER

❋ A BOOK YOU LIKE

Isn't it weird that nobody has the exact same voice? It doesn't take long to recognize a bud's voice—with one word, you know exactly who it is. Uniqueness is just one of the many cool things about your voice.

Learning how and when to use your voice definitely has its benefits. With a strong, clear voice you can convince people that you're cool and confident, even if you're shaking in your boots. Ever told a super-funny joke and nobody laughed? Could be a voice thing.

With the right voice, you can make just about anything sound pretty darn funny. Some people—standup comics and actors who do animated movies—make careers out of manipulating their voices. Who knows? Your voice could be worth millions!

How to Speak Like a Pro:

✿ Record yourself reading from a magazine or book.

✿ Play back the tape. It might sound freaky—most folks cringe at the sound of their own voice—but don't let that stop you!

✿ If something about your voice bugs you, work on changing it.

- If your voice sounds too high, put the book on the floor, and practice reading from it, face down. Your voice will be lower. Sit upright and speak in that same lower pitch.

- If your voice is too soft, raise your voice to a louder level. Pretend you're the lead role of a play, and you need your voice to carry out to the whole audience.

- If your speech sounds strained, yawn and talk at the same time to relax your throat.

Once you're satisfied, do some experimenting. Read the same passage in a quiet voice, a loud voice, a scary voice, a baby's voice, etc. Read, record, and listen to the tape until you have a grasp of your range—or, just goof off! Maybe make a couple calls with your new Southern belle voice....

Chapter 2

Makeover Madness

Go ahead and revel in a little vanity, girlfriend! Primp, crimp, curl, twirl, scrub, buff, deep-condition, dab, and apply. Spin soft music, burn some lavender incense, and have a perfectly fabulous pamper-your-pretty-self spa-at-home day. Or, get with a bunch of buds for a blow-out beautifying bash. Either way, you'll be gorgeously glam and feeling fantastically refreshed.

Give Your 'Do a New Vibe

What You'll Need:
* ❋ AN OLD PAIR OF JEANS
* ❋ SCISSORS
* ❋ RULER

Blue jean curls! They're soft, natural-looking coily-cues that can give any 'do of any length a new lease on life. To make 'em all over your head, follow these instructions:

1. First, chop up a pair of old trashed jeans! Why? Because blue jean "curlers" are simply strips of denim. Cut a bunch of denim strips that are about 4-inches long and 1-inch wide each.

2. Wash and condition your hair as usual.

3. While your hair is still damp, make a rag curl by wrapping about a 1-inch section of your hair in a tight coil pattern (like you'd twist your hair in a curler) around a denim strip. Leave the ends of the denim free.

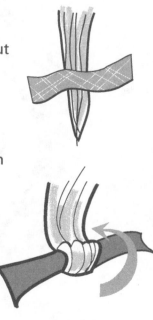

4. Tie the ends of the strip together, pulling your hair close to your head. The tighter you tie your "curler," the tighter your curl will be.

5. Repeat all over your head, or wherever you want to create luscious bounce.

6. Sleep with the denim ties in overnight. Don't worry—they're WAY more comfy than regular rollers!

7. In the morning, untie your blue jean curlers, and behold—blue jean curls! Separate and comb your curls with your fingers only— don't brush or your head will be a big poof!

Crimp Your Style

What You'll Need:
* ❄ A BAG OF SMALL ELASTIC PONYTAIL HOLDERS OR RUBBER BANDS
* ❄ A SPRAY BOTTLE FILLED WITH WATER

Crimped hair looks amazing—like a million adorable little waves all over your head! If you've got hair that's shoulder length or longer, this do-it-yourself-'do is really fun to try.

It's easy to crimp your hair, but be warned—it can be time-consuming. (The more hair you've got, the longer it will take.) We recommend you start a couple of hours before bedtime.

Here's How:

1. Wet your hair fully, then start making very tiny braids all over your head.

2. Use the spray bottle to respritz your hair with water, if it starts to dry.

3. Once you've got a headful of braids, hit the sack, leaving them in overnight. In the morning, take down all of the braids—and your hair will be perfectly crimped!

4. Finger-comb your hair to separate the waves—DO NOT brush your hair! The look will last till your next shampoo.

Have an All-You-Can-Wear Contest   Just for Fun

Grab a couple of friends and a pile of clothes. Start by wearing only bathing suits, and then see how many clothes you can put on in five minutes. The person with the most items of clothing on at the end wins!

Give Your Poor Frizzed-Out Hair a Deep Conditioning Treatment

What You'll Need:

* ❋ 1/2 CUP OF CONDITIONER
* ❋ 1/4 CUP OF HONEY
* ❋ 1 TABLESPOON OF ALMOND OIL
  (LOOK IN THE SALAD DRESSING SECTION OF A GROCERY STORE)
* ❋ A WIDE-TOOTH COMB
* ❋ A PLASTIC SHOWER CAP
* ❋ A BATH TOWEL

Is your hair going crazy with static? Are your ends splitting like dry spaghetti? Is your overall 'do a dry, lifeless don't? Well, you're not alone. The solution? Treat your tresses to some much-needed deep conditioning.

1. Wash your hair with a moisture-rich shampoo. Lather only once; rinse twice.

2. Towel dry gently, then comb all tangles and snarlies out of your hair.

3. Mix the conditioner, honey, and almond oil together. Now, starting at the roots of your hair, use your fingers to smooth and coat your hair evenly with the conditioner mix, working all the way down the length.

4. Comb through your hair again to make sure the conditioner is spread through completely.

5. Gather up your hair and secure it under the shower cap.

6. Now chill out for the next twenty to thirty minutes, letting that conditioner soak in and do its hair repair magic.

7. Time's up! Rinse all of the conditioner out of your hair.

8. Towel dry again—very, very gently. Let your hair air dry— the end result will be a head of to-die-for silky strands!

Up Your Hair's Shine Factor

What You'll Need:

* ❋ YOUR FAVE SHAMPOO
* ❋ A TOWEL
* ❋ A SPOONFUL OF PLAIN VINEGAR
* ❋ A SMALL AMOUNT OF CONDITIONER

Want sparkly, glossy, gleaming hair? Then rev up its shine by giving it a vinegar rinse. Amazingly, a spoonful of that stinky stuff does wonders to tired hair!

1. Drizzle vinegar onto clean, towel-dried hair and scrunch hair from roots to ends.

2. Let the vinegar settle into your hair for fifteen to twenty minutes.

3. Rinse out the vinegar.

4. Now apply a small amount of conditioner to your hair (so that your hair won't smell like vinegar) and rinse again.

5. Blow-dry and style your hair as usual. Then be careful not to blind people with those shiny strands!

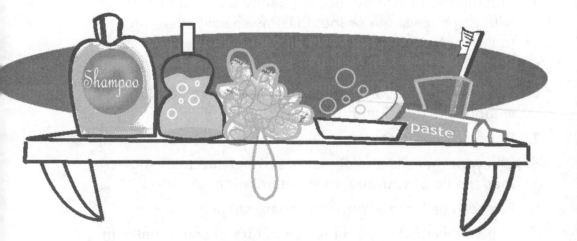

Pretty Pedicure

What You'll Need:

* ❊ NAIL POLISH REMOVER AND COTTON BALLS
* ❊ A BASIN OF WARM, SOAPY WATER
* ❊ A PUMICE STONE OR FOOT FILE
* ❊ A FOOT SCRUB (LIKE PEPPERMINT FOOT LOTION)
* ❊ A SOFT TOWEL
* ❊ NAIL CLIPPERS
* ❊ A NAIL FILE
* ❊ TOE-SEPARATORS, COTTON BALLS, OR TOILET PAPER
* ❊ A SHIMMERY NAIL POLISH
* ❊ A BOTTLE OF CLEAR TOP COAT

Whether it's sandal season or not, treat your tootsies to a refreshing and shimmery pedicure!

1. Remove any old polish from your toes with cotton balls and nail polish remover.

2. Place your feet in the tub of soapy, warm water and soak for ten glorious minutes.

3. Remove your feet from the tub, but don't dry them.

4. Smooth rough skin by rubbing gently but vigorously with a pumice stone or foot file. Pay special attention to the heels and soles of your feet.

5. Return your feet to the tub and soak for one more minute.

6. Remove your feet and lather up with a foot scrub to smooth any remaining rough skin.

7. Rinse and completely dry off your feet.

8. Clip your toenails straight across. Don't cut them shorter than the tip of your toe, to avoid irritation.

9. File each nail into a rounded-square shape.

10. Separate your toes with toe-separators or cotton balls, or weave toilet paper through each toe for easier polishing.

11. Apply two coats of your shimmery polish to your toes, then let the polish dry thoroughly.

12. Apply one layer of top coat to seal your pedicure, let it dry again, and admire those perfect piggies!

An Italian Manicure!

SOLO

What You'll Need:

* COTTON BALLS AND NAIL POLISH REMOVER
* A NAIL FILE
* A BOTTLE OF CLEAR NAIL POLISH
* A BOTTLE OF DARK RED NAIL POLISH

Want the scoop on a hot European trend? Started in Italy and spotted on supermodels, this nail 'do will make your digits look long, slender, and gorgeous.

1. Remove any old polish from your nails with cotton balls and nail polish remover.

2. File each nail into a rounded-square shape.

3. Paint a base coat of clear polish on each nail. Let it dry.

4. Now, *veeeery* carefully, paint a thin vertical stripe of dark red polish down the center of each nail. Leave the rest of each nail color-free. Let your nails dry completely.

5. Finish up with a top coat. *Bella!* (That's "beautiful" in Italian, in case you didn't know.)

Down-to-Earth Face Mask

SOLO

What You'll Need:

- **2 TABLESPOONS OF UNCOOKED OLD-FASHIONED OATMEAL** (NOT INSTANT)
- **1/2 CUP OF WARM WATER**
- **A SMALL BOWL FOR MIXING YOUR MASK**
- **A SPOON**
- **A TOWEL**

Get your skin glowing with this fresh face mask! Whip it up as follows:

1. Combine the uncooked oatmeal and warm water in a bowl.
2. Mix the ingredients vigorously with your spoon until it's a thick paste.
3. Before applying, pull your hair back away from your face. Then, with your hands, spread the paste all over your face (avoid your eyes).
4. Leave the mask on for fifteen minutes.
5. Rinse your face with warm water and pat dry.

Give Yourself a Steam Facial

SOLO

What You'll Need:

- **A HANDFUL OF THE AROMATHERAPY OF YOUR CHOICE** (SEE BELOW)
- **A COUPLE OF TOWELS**

Keep your skin gorgeous by giving yourself a steam facial. For dry skin, add dried lavender or mint (available at health food stores). For sensitive skin, toss in dried chamomile (available in tea bags in the tea aisle of your grocery store). For oily skin, add rose petals and witchhazel (available at drug stores and grocery stores). Here's how:

1. Go into the bathroom, and close the door tightly.
2. Fill up the sink with super-hot water. Toss in some herbs.
3. Put a towel over your head, and lean your face over the sink for five minutes. Be careful not to let your face touch the hot water.
4. When you're finished, gently pat your face dry.

Take Center Stage

It's show time! You could bring down the house with an amazing performance, but who says an audience is always necessary? You can entertain yourself quite nicely with a solo act. Bravo! Somebody, get that girl an agent!

The Making of a Superstar: What's Your Movie Star Name?

WITH A GROUP OF BUDS

What You'll Need:
* A LITTLE CREATIVITY
* A LITTLE GLAM

Dream of becoming the next Gwyneth, Reese, or Cameron? If so, get your act together and give yourself a Hollywood-worthy name. You'll need a one-of-a-kind name that screams superstar! After all, most of the A-listers don't use their real names. Meg Ryan's real name is Margaret Hyra. Tom Cruise wasn't born Tom Cruise—he started life as Thomas Mapother IV. Life as a star can be tough, but creating your star name is a synch!

Here's one equation: Name of Spice + Name of Car = Movie Star Name

Don't say why, just ask your buds to name their favorite spice (Ginger, Rosemary, Nutmeg, etc). Have friends name a kind of car (Ford, Cadillac, Lincoln, etc). Try using a flower, alternatively, for either your first or last name.

Put the two names together, like, Ginger Ford or Rosemary Cadillac. *Voilà!* Now *that's* a movie star name! You're on your way to the silver screen, sister!

Master Magic!

SOLO, THEN IN FRONT OF AN AUDIENCE!

What You'll Need:
* THE POWERS OF THE UNIVERSE

Amaze your parents! Dazzle your friends! Who doesn't love magic? Spend an afternoon perfecting these tricks. Then try them out on your friends or family!

WHAT KNOT?

What You'll Need:
* A SCARF AND SOME FLEXIBLE FINGERS

What You Do:

1. Fold two corners of the scarf together so your scarf takes on a triangular shape. Lay the scarf so that the long straight edge is at the top and the point is in front of you. Then, starting at the point, roll the scarf away from you into a ropelike thickness and shape.

Step 2

Step 3

2. Hold the ends of the rolled-up scarf between your index and middle fingers on each hand.

3. If you're right handed, take the end in your right hand and place it between the thumb and index finger of your left hand. The scarf should be making a loop in your left hand (your right hand should be free).

4. With your right hand, grab the loop, and stick it between the middle and third finger on your left hand. Again, with your right hand, take hold of the end that's between the index and middle fingers of your left hand. Gently pull it through the loop. You should start to see something that looks like a knot forming over the middle finger on your left hand. (Lefties, do the reverse so the knot starts to form over the middle finger on your right hand.)

Step 4

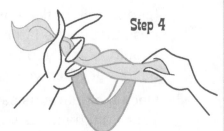

Step 5

Step 6

5. When the "knot" is close to your fingers, let go of the scarf with your right hand and hold up the scarf for your audience to see.

6. Quickly yank on both ends of the scarf. The "knot" should disappear!

THE FRENCH DROP

What You'll Need:
✳ **A QUARTER AND A POCKET**

What You Do:

1. Hold a quarter in your right hand, palm up, with the coin between your thumb and first two fingers. Slip the thumb of your left hand under the quarter, and close your fingers around the coin, as if you're taking it in your left hand.

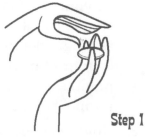

Step 1

2. Instead, drop the quarter into your right hand. While secretly slipping the quarter into a pocket on your right side (a sweater or jeans pocket), swing your left arm up, keeping your left hand in a fist (people will notice this motion and miss that you're hiding the quarter!). Everyone should expect you to have the quarter in your left hand, but when you open your fist, it's empty!

Step 2

3. Once the quarter is safely in your pocket, open your right hand, as well. Ooooh—both hands are empty!

Step 3

Do As I Do

What You'll Need:
✳ **2 DECKS OF CARDS**

What You Do:

1. Hold one deck of cards, and give another to your friend. Tell your friend to do exactly as you do.

2. Shuffle your pack.

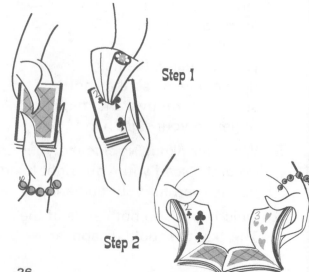

Step 1

Step 2

26

3. Exchange packs and shuffle again.

4. Switch packs once more, but this time, as you begin to shuffle, sneak a peek (very inconspicuously) at the bottom card in your deck before handing it over again. Tell your friend to remove any card from her deck, and to place that card on top of her deck once she's memorized it.

5. You pretend to do the same. Remove a card, act like you're memorizing it, but really remember only the card you just saw on the bottom of your friend's deck.

6. Now both of you should cut your decks once.

7. Then exchange decks one last time.

8. Fan through your cards, looking for the one you memorized. You'll find your friend's card immediately to the right of the one you remembered. Your friend will be surprised when the card you pull out is the one she chose!

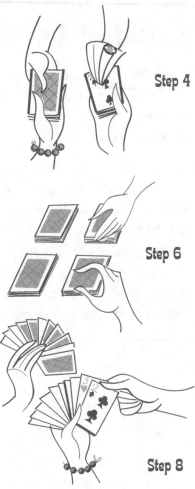

Step 4

Step 6

Step 8

Hand Jive

What You'll Need:
   * A GREASE DVD OR VIDEOTAPE
   * A BIG, BARE ROOM WITH A BIG, BARE FLOOR

You gotta love Sandy, Danny, Rizzo, and of course the gang's groovy Hand Jive! If you're hanging with the girls, pop the flick in, let loose, and have a ball doing the hand jive! And with a little practice, you all will be talent-show winners in no time flat! Just think how much fun it'd be to sport a poodle skirt and hand jive across the stage!

Sing Along with *The Sound of Music*

What You'll Need:
* *THE SOUND OF MUSIC* ON DVD OR VHS
* A PEN
* SOME PAPER

There's a scary-wonderful phenomenon that's been growing over the past couple of years—first in England, and now in America. People are flocking to movie theaters to watch *The Sound of Music*, and sing along to all its groovy tunes via onscreen subtitles. We are so there!

Pop in the DVD or VHS, and fast-forward till you hit a musical number, then jot down the lyrics and make copies so your buds can join in! Put in the movie and start warbling. Recommended refreshments: Tea...to drink with jam and bread!

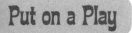

Put on a Play

What You'll Need:
* ✳ **A SPACE TO PERFORM YOUR PLAY**
* ✳ **A SCRIPT**

Are you a natural ham who loves to do impressions and act out scenes from your favorite flicks? Or are you more of a behind-the-scenes person—do you like to write stories and skits? Why not put your talents to great use and stage your own play production?

You can write your own play, if you're so inclined—or stage your own version of a favorite story or play. Ask permission to use the stage or a large classroom at school to put on the production, or use someone's large living room for a more local performance. Cast your buds—or hold auditions among your classmates.

Direct the play yourself. You can do it! The first time out, just keep things simple. No fancy lighting, costumes, or sets. Just let your pure talent, and the talent of your cast, shine through—keep that in mind, and your show will be a smashing success!

Start an All-girl Band

What You'll Need:
* ✳ **INSTRUMENTS** (IF YOU PLAY ANY)
* ✳ **YOUR VOICES** (IF YOU DON'T)

You and your crew can start your own rockin' all-girl band in an afternoon. If you love singing and if any of you play instruments already, you're good to go. (Your average, solid pop band setup includes a lead singer, a guitar player, a bass player, a keyboard player, and a drummer.) But even if you don't play an instrument, don't despair. Have you ever heard songs with really good harmony? Try it. Blended together, your voices will sound amazing—even *a cappella* (that's Italian for, "without any instruments accompanying the singing").

Start a Dance Craze

WITH A GROUP OF BUDS

What You'll Need:

- A LITTLE NERVE

It's Friday night, and here you are at yet another *booooooring* school dance. The music's slammin', but the problem is the dancing leaves a lot to be desired. Everybody's just kind of bopping up and down, doing the same dull moves you've seen a million times before.

You love to dance, and it just so happens that you learned a fab new hip-hop twist on the electric slide last weekend at your cousin's wedding. Why not bust a move right here, right now? A new dance craze will spread all over the gym like wildfire—all you need to do is get the ball rolling.

Avoid getting dissed by any random losers by teaching the dance to your girls in a corner first, then head out onto the dance floor to do it as a group. Start moving, and before you know it, other kids will join in! The gym will be rocking in no time—thanks to you, the life o' the party.

Compose Your Own Lyrics

SOLO OR WITH A BUD

What You'll Need:

- A TAPE RECORDER AND A TAPE
- AN INSTRUMENT, LIKE A GUITAR OR KEYBOARD (OPTIONAL)

Are you constantly humming melodies under your breath? Do you have a knack for writing a good line of poetry? If so, why not try writing your own song? To bust out a groovin' tune, you just have to be willing to have fun and experiment.

You may think that songwriting is way complicated. Don't you need to know how to play a bazillion instruments, have perfect pitch and natural-born singing skill to pull it off? Not at all. Here's the easy-peasy route to crafting a tune in an afternoon!

Either on your own or with a partner, plop down in a quiet, comfy spot, like your room. Think of a subject. ANY subject—it doesn't need to be super profound. You can write a song about your dog, the sky, a wastebasket—you name it.

Now jot down some rhymin' lyrics about the topic. If the subject of your song is silly, feel free to be funny. If you feel the need to write a song about something more meaningful—like the friendship you feel for your BFF or the boy you're crushing on—the best thing to do is to be honest and just express your feelings. You don't have to mention names in your song, or ultimately even share it with anybody else— the song you write should be for you, first and foremost.

Write a verse, then a chorus, then another verse, then repeat your chorus. Here's a guideline you can follow:

VERSE

I was hungry as a big brown bear
I was lookin' for fast food everywhere!
I was about to pull out my hair
When suddenly, I became aware—

CHORUS

Of the Golden Arches!
I saw the Golden Arches!
Now whenever I crave a snack
Or suffer a bad Big Mac Attack
I hit the Golden Arches!

VERSE

"French Fry" is my middle name
McNuggets are my claim to fame
I've loved McDonald's chow so long
And I had to tell you in this song!

REPEAT CHORUS

To come up with a funky melody, just relax and let loose. If you *do* play an instrument, noodle around with melody ideas that might fit your lyrics. If you don't know how to play an instrument or write music, no biggie. Just play around with singing your lines. When you like what you've come up with, sing into your tape recorder so you won't forget your melody.

Now practice singing your lyrics to your melody over and over till you've got it down pat. Tweak or rewrite the words or music however you want, until you're totally satisfied with your song. The final step: Record your completed creation on its own special tape! Beware: Songwriting is habit-forming. Once you've written one tune, chances are you'll instantly have oodles of ideas for more!

Host a Radio Show!

WITH A GROUP OF BUDS

What You'll Need:
* A TAPE RECORDER
* TAPE

Make your own radio show with your buds. Using a cassette tape recorder, put on your own unique broadcast. You can make up hilarious commercials for weird household products (doggie breath mints, anyone?), interview each other, and play your favorite songs, just like a real station does. Use weird sound effects that you can invent around the house—clang pots and pans, use a buzzing egg timer or alarm clock to announce the time, or anything else you can think up!

Chapter 4

Fun with Friends

your posse, your *amigas*, or your gal pals! It's hard to imagine what you'd do without them...especially when you imagine all that you can do *with* them. The fun is always multiplied when you mix it with all your chicks.

Make Your Own Slambook

What You'll Need:
* ✳ A NOTEBOOK
* ✳ MATERIALS FOR DECORATION
* ✳ A BUNCH OF PENS

Molly likes to draw, and Julie loves soccer. Kristi makes awesome cookies, and Bridget can get lost in a good book. Surely, you could rattle off a list of your friends' likes and dislikes—and they know yours. But have you ever sat down together and asked each other questions you really had to think about before answering? If you haven't, this is a perfect opportunity to make a slambook!

Take a blank notebook, and decorate the cover so that it represents you and your friends. You could cut out magazine pictures or your favorite quotes, and glue them on, for example. Now, it's time to fill in the slambook. Make the first page the sign-in page, where each person chooses a symbol that really expresses who she is (like a soccer ball or gingerbread cookie) and fills in her name. Then, on the top of each page, write a posing question, silly or serious—what you ask is up to you. Need a few questions to get you going? Try some of the ones below!

* ❀ If you could only eat one food for the rest of your life, what would it be?
* ❀ Name one gift you've always wanted but have never received.
* ❀ What happened in the last year that made you laugh the hardest?
* ❀ What color resembles your personality the most and why?
* ❀ Name one secret you hide from your parents.

Once you've filled out the answers to the questions on your page, your buds are next. Pass the book along, having each person fill it out. When all of you are finished, sit together and share your answers.

Let it Snowglobe, Let it Snowglobe, Let it Snowglobe!

What You'll Need:

- ✳ ONE SMALL, CLEAR JAR
- ✳ SUPERGLUE
- ✳ A SMALL PLASTIC FIGURE
- ✳ SOME WATER
- ✳ FINE GLITTER
- ✳ MATERIALS FOR DECORATION (OPTIONAL)

No snow? No problem! Here's your chance to make it snow anytime you want, in your very own snowglobe!

1. Take a clean, clear jar, remove the lid and use some Superglue to attach a plastic figure to the underside of the lid.

2. While that's drying, fill the jar with water (over a sink)—leaving just a tiny bit of space so that the water doesn't overflow when you put your figure into it.

3. Then, add some glitter as snow.

4. When the jar lid is dry, very tightly attach it to your jar. Decorate the outside of the jar, if you like.

5. Now, flip your snow globe over so the jar is upside down—you just made it snow!

EXTRA TIP: If you're feeling ambitious, you can decorate the sides of the lid with construction paper, extra glitter, sequins, ribbon, or beads.

Go on a Scavenger Hunt!

What You'll Need:
❋ **A GROOVY LIST OF ITEMS TO HIDE** (ONE COPY FOR EACH PLAYER)

You don't have to look far for a guaranteed good time if you organize a scavenger hunt! If you've never been on a scavenger hunt, here's the basic idea: You and your buds break into random teams (like by drawing numbers from a hat), and each team is given a list of things to do or find in a limited amount of time. Each item on the list has a different point value. So, the harder something is to find—like a dog with a purple collar—the higher the point value. The team who returns to the finish line with the most stuff from the list wins!

Hunt Specifics:

✿ Ideally, you want to plan ahead and have your to-find lists already written out. Might be best to have a parent organize the hunt so everyone can participate. If you come up with the list of stuff to find, you can't participate...'cause that's not fair!

✿ You can hide stuff just before the hunt, or you can send people out in search of stuff you haven't planted (like a pinecone or a Pepsi can). Once again, whoever hides stuff can't "play."

✿ You want at least three teams with 3–5 pals per team. But, there's no reason you can't have a hunt with fewer or more people, just make necessary team adjustments.

✿ Each team gets one copy of the list. Make sure point values are next to each item. The rules must be clear to each team and it's best to include any rules on the list, too.

✿ *Boundaries:* Make sure everyone is clear on the boundaries—like teams can only search within a specific block or from your house to your friend Hannah's. Also, make sure at least one person from each team is familiar with the neighborhood so nobody gets lost or confused!

✿ *Time Limit:* All teams start at the same place at the same time, and all teams need to return to the same place at the same time.

✿ *Off-limits:* If certain places are off-limits, make sure everyone knows. It's usually best to make participants' houses off-limits (that's too easy).

✿ If pals have digital cameras they can bring along, instruct teams to take pictures of their findings. This works especially well if you want them to scavenger for something that doesn't quite fit in a bag. Like a fire engine or a man walking a baby! Otherwise, just arm each team with a grocery bag.

✿ Whoever was in charge of making the scavenger list must inventory each group's bag and add up points as they return. That person can also disqualify things if they "don't count." Like if all groups were supposed to find a Pepsi can and a group returned with a Coke can, that person would decide if the Coke does or doesn't count.

✿ Plan ahead and make sure the winning team is rewarded with a prize (gift certificates to your local ice cream place, goodie bags with fun candy, lip gloss, etc). Or, ask each participant to contribute like $5–$10, and then the winning team gets to split all the booty!

Some ideas of what to find:

A PENNY FROM 1999

A PIECE OF JUICY FRUIT GUM OR GUM WRAPPER

A DOG BONE

A PURPLE CRAYON

THAT DAY'S NEWSPAPER

A TAKEOUT MENU

A BUMPER STICKER WITH THE U.S. FLAG

A FEATHER

THE PHONE NUMBER TO YOUR LOCAL LIBRARY

A MAP OF YOUR TOWN

MONOPOLY MONEY

A NEW TENNIS BALL

A POLICE OFFICER'S SIGNATURE

P.S. Of course, your list needs to take the time of year into account. No fair asking teams to find dandelions in October!

Go Berry Picking

What You'll Need:

＊ A SMALL ADMISSION FEE

Many farms allow paying customers to stroll their grounds, picking all the blueberries, strawberries, raspberries, or blackberries that can fit into one basket (or ten). Take advantage of such a *ripe* opportunity to stock up on your favorite fruits. Once you and your buds have picked all the berries you can, take them home and clean them (Mom can give you the head's up on the how-to's). What do you do with your bounty? Make muffins!

BERRY MUFFINS

What You'll Need:

＊ 1-1/2 CUPS OF ALL-PURPOSE FLOUR
＊ 3/4 CUP OF WHITE SUGAR
＊ 1/2 TEASPOON OF SALT
＊ 2 TEASPOONS OF BAKING POWDER
＊ 1/3 CUP OF VEGETABLE OIL
＊ 1 EGG
＊ 1/3 CUP OF MILK
＊ 1 CUP OF FRESH BLUEBERRIES, RASPBERRIES, BLACKBERRIES, OR STRAWBERRIES
＊ AN ADULT FOR HELP
＊ YOU'LL ALSO NEED A MUFFIN PAN, MUFFIN LINERS, A LARGE MIXING BOWL, MEASURING CUPS, A MEDIUM MIXING BOWL, A WOODEN SPOON, A SPATULA, AND A FORK

For Crumb Topping:

＊ 1/2 CUP OF WHITE SUGAR
＊ 1/3 CUP OF ALL-PURPOSE FLOUR
＊ 1/4 CUP OF BUTTER, CUBED
＊ 1-1/2 TEASPOONS OF GROUND CINNAMON

What You Do:

Preheat the oven to 400 degrees. Grease a muffin pan or line it with muffin liners. Combine the flour, sugar, salt, and baking powder in a large bowl. Place the vegetable oil into a medium bowl, along with the egg and milk. Then, pour the "wet" mixture into the flour mixture and stir. Fold in the berries. Fill each muffin cup to the top, and sprinkle with the crumb topping. Bake for 20 to 25 minutes or until done.

To make crumb topping: Mix the sugar, flour, butter, and cinnamon with a fork, and sprinkle over muffins before baking.

Bob for Apples

What You'll Need:

* ✸ APPLES
* ✸ A BIG TUB, FILLED WITH WATER, WIDE ENOUGH TO PUT YOUR HEAD IN

Nothing says Fall fun like bobbing for apples, although you can have fun with apples any time of year. Try these variations on this crazy water sport:

* ✿ **Lead with your chin:** Try to pick up an apple with the underside of your chin, pressing and holding it to your chest till you've got one completely out of the water (just like how you pass oranges in relay races).

* ✿ **Speed-bobbing:** See who can be the first to snag an apple in ten seconds.

* ✿ **Hi, Bob!:** Everybody repeats the phrase, "Hi, Bob!" over and over again as fast as possible while trying to, well, bob. It's tougher than it sounds.

Board Game Marathon

What You'll Need:

* ✸ EVERY BOARD GAME EVER CREATED

Monopoly! Scrabble! Password! Twister! Even Candyland! Calling all board game fans: Ask your crew to bring over their board game collections for a board game marathon! The more, the merrier! Set up games all over the room, and break into pairs or teams. When you're finished with one game, just move on to the next, till you simply cannot pass "GO" one more time. Keep running scores to determine the ultimate board game champs!

Play Challenge Games with Your Friends — Just for Fun

For example, how many girl names can you think of that begin with the letter L? How many boy names? Play in teams or one on one.

Make a Time Capsule

What You'll Need:
- ❈ TIME CAPSULE TREASURES
- ❈ A METAL BOX, LIKE A SMALL SAFE OR CASH BOX

Let your legend live on! Preserve a piece of yourself for the future. Gather with a group of buds and stash your memories away for future generations, alien invaders, or whomever might come across your treasure trove. Or, agree to dig up your time capsule, say, the year you graduate from high school! Seriously, it will be a total crack up!

You want to include stuff that'll remind you guys about what was going on when you made your time capsule! So, add a copy of a current newspaper or weekly mag. Also, include pictures, CD's, notes to yourselves, memories about your friends. Just make sure NOT to include anything perishable—you don't want to be greeted by moldy gummy worms when you decide to crack your time capsule open. Agree on a safe place to bury your capsule, like under the elm in your yard or in your attic, and vow to unearth it the day you graduate!

Try Sumo Wrestling

What You'll Need:
- ❈ TWO BED PILLOWS

Let's give props to the ancient Japanese sport/art form of sumo wrestling—you saw it on the big screen in *Charlie's Angels*! Wanna try it yourself? Grab a pillow, stuff it under your shirt and over your stomach (secure it in your pants waistband if it fits), and wrestle your BFF or sis! C'mon, get silly!

Chapter 5

Great Get-Togethers

Sure, hanging with the crew is fun, but sometimes you want to go all out. Here are our favorite tips for throwing the best bash. Be the talk of the town, the hostess with the mostest, Miss Socialite Extraordinaire, the princess of party planning. So, what are you waiting for? Start sending those invites out!

Host a Sunrise (Sleepover) Surprise

What You'll Need:

 ❋ A GOOD VIEW OF THE HORIZON

Sleepovers are all about staying up late and sleeping in, right? Not always! Set an alarm just before sunrise—which will depend on where you live and the time of year, but usually it's around 5:30 or 6:00. It won't kill ya, we promise. Have everyone crawl out of bed, and point themselves at the horizon—the view may be good enough from your bedroom window. (If not, put on some jeans and a T, and go outside.) Give Mother Nature a few minutes to rub the sleep out of her eyes— then get ready for a beautiful, flame-colored sun to shoot into the sky. Wow! Isn't that cool? Everyone will be thrilled you got them up early. Or maybe not. If not, head back to bed for a few hours. Then serve...

CHOCOLATE CHIP "WAKE UP" PANCAKES

What You'll Need:

 ❋ 2 CUPS OF FLOUR

 ❋ 3 TEASPOONS OF BAKING POWDER

 ❋ 1/4 CUP OF SUGAR

 ❋ 1/2 TEASPOON OF SALT

 ❋ 1 CUP OF MILK

 ❋ 2 TABLESPOONS OF OIL

 ❋ 2 EGGS

 ❋ 1 BAG OF CHOCOLATE CHIPS

 ❋ AN ADULT FOR SOME NECESSARY HELP

 ❋ ONE LARGE BOWL, MEASURING CUPS AND MEASURING SPOONS, A WOODEN SPOON, A NONSTICK FRYING PAN (OR A REGULAR FRYING PAN SPRAYED WITH COOKING OIL SO THE PANCAKES DON'T STICK)

Sure, the sleepover last night was a blast, but make the next morning fun, too (especially since you just got everyone up only a few hours after they went to sleep)! Or, try something new—if you haven't had a sleepover the night before, invite your friends over in the morning (tell them there's no need to change out of their pajamas!) to do something extra special together, like making chocolate chip pancakes from scratch!

Don't forget to have some tasty pancake toppings on hand, like whipped cream, powdered sugar, and maple syrup to jazz up your breakfast even more!

What You Do:

1. Measure out all of the dry ingredients (flour, baking powder, sugar, and salt) and then combine them in a large bowl. Use your wooden spoon to mix them slightly.

2. Measure out the liquid ingredients (milk, oil, and eggs), and then stir them into the dry ingredients in the large bowl, until most of the lumps are gone.

3. Pour some chocolate chips (as few or as many as you like) into the pancake batter and stir once more.

4. Ask an adult to help you heat the frying pan. When the frying pan is hot, fill your ladle half-full with pancake batter and pour onto the frying pan.

5. With an adult's help, cook each pancake until its underside is light brown and the top is bubbly. Then flip the pancake over with the spatula until the other side is light brown as well.

6. Repeat the directions above, until you've used all of the batter and you have a tower of pancakes to share with your buds.

TIP: Uninspired by the traditional, round pancake shape? Try setting a metal cookie cutter on your frying pan (never use plastic, they'll melt onto your pan!). Then, pour the pancake batter into the center of the cookie cutter—and leave the cookie cutter in place until the pancake is ready to be flipped. Now have an adult carefully remove the cutter (the metal might be a bit toasty in places). Use all kinds of shapes like hearts, triangles, and letters to give your chocolate chip pancakes a little flash!

Throw a Surprise Party (And Serve Baby-sized Cakes)

What You'll Need:
* ✳ PARTY SUPPLIES
* ✳ THE ABILITY TO BLUFF
* ✳ BUDS WHO CAN KEEP A SECRET

You don't have to wait till a friend's birthday to throw her a surprise party! Has she just earned her tenth merit badge in Girl Scouts? Is she going away for the summer to see her grandma? Has she been feeling a little down lately, and could use a happy day? These are all totally legit reasons to celebrate her mega-coolness!

Throw it alone or cut costs and up the fun by getting your other buds involved, serve her favorite foods, and you're good to go! Your bud will always remember how thoughtful you were.

BABY-SIZED CAKES

What You'll Need:
* ✳ TWO SMALL-SIZE (LIKE 4-INCH) ROUND CAKE PANS
* ✳ YOUR FAVE CAKE MIX AND TUB OF ICING
* ✳ TOOTHPICKS, A WOODEN SPOON, MEASURING CUPS, AND MEASURING SPOONS
* ✳ TUBES OF COLORED FROSTING AND FROSTING GELS
* ✳ DECORATIONS LIKE GUMMY BEARS, SPRINKLES, THOSE EDIBLE LITTLE SILVER BALL THINGS, RED HOTS, COLORED SUGAR, ANIMAL CRACKERS, GUM DROPS, ROPE LICORICE, AND CANDLES

What You Do:

Use small-sized cake molds, instead of the normal 8- or 9-inch cake pans. Cook at the normal temperature specified in your cake mix's instructions, but reduce the cooking time by half. Watch your baby-sized cakes extra carefully so they don't burn or get too over done. (Remember to do the toothpick test—have an adult stick a toothpick in the center of the cakes. When the toothpick comes out with crumbs, not raw batter, it's done.)

Let the cakes cool, then layer and frost as usual. Then get decorating! Write your bud's initials on the cake, do a theme cake (all pink perhaps?) or just make them as cute as cute can be. And, of course, don't forget just one little candle apiece.

Host a Swap Session!

WITH A GROUP OF BUDS

What You'll Need:
  * UNWANTED STUFF YOU'VE HAD STASHED IN THE CORNERS OF YOUR ROOM AND CLOSET

Is your closet groaning under the weight of jeans you no longer wear, Beanie Babies you're totally over, and snow boots that pinch your toes? Sounds like it's time for a Swap Session!

Here's How a Swap Session Works:

1. Clear out your closet, drawers and shelves, removing all the things you no longer want—but that might still be fun for to someone else.

2. Invite your buds to do the same and send out invites for an official swap-party.

3. Gather in the living room, spread out all the goodies (keeping everyone's stuff in its own area so it's easy to tell whose stuff is whose).

4. Go around the room and take turns trading! Trade until everyone has traded all they can. Or, until you're left with stuff nobody can even *give* away! Pack up the leftover stuff and donate it to the Salvation Army or a homeless shelter.

Have a yaD sdrawkcaB (Backwards Day) Just for Fun

Do everything backwards one day. After a sleepover with a friend, do everything backwards. Talk backwards, eat backwards (starting with dessert first), wear your clothes backwards, etc. Have dinner for breakfast and breakfast for dinner. See how much fun it can be.

Welcome a New Friend

What You'll Need:

❈ SOME REALLY DELICIOUS TAKEOUT OR A HOMEMADE CROWD PLEASER LUNCH

❈ A COLORFUL LUNCH TABLE, SET WITH SUPER-FUN PARTY FAVORS

❈ CUPS, PLATES, PLASTIC UTENSILS

❈ A HUGE, HANDMADE "WELCOME!" BANNER

❈ A DVD PLAYER OR A VCR

❈ A GOOD DVD OR VIDEOTAPE

❈ SOME BOARD GAMES

You know that cool new girl you've noticed at lunch, at the pool, or at the bus stop? Why not welcome her to your neck of the woods! A great way? Throw her a Saturday lunch party!

A lunch party is a good choice when you're first getting to know a new friend. Invite as many kids as your folks will allow, and ask if you can serve tasty takeout that you know everybody's going to enjoy— like sub sandwiches or pizza. Make a big "WELCOME!" sign, and have all of your friends sign it.

Plan a few fun games for after lunch, or watch a fun movie. No doubt your new bud will be happy, flattered, and impressed that you were so thoughtful from the get-go!

46

Have a Jeopardy-style Study Session

What You'll Need:

* YOUR CLASS NOTES
* INDEX CARDS
* CARDBOARD TO MAKE A GAME BOARD
* MAGIC MARKERS
* A FUN LITTLE PRIZE

Sweating that history quiz next week? Get prepped the fun way by holding a Jeopardy study sesh. Do it just like the game show we all know and love. Write up subject questions, one to an index card. Then make a game board with related titles—like: *By George! (Washington)*; *Honest Like Abe (Lincoln)*; *Famous Speeches in History*—you get the picture.

Call up your classmates, and have everybody over for a game—right before your test, once everyone's had a chance to get familiar with the study material. The winner gets a prize, like a cool new CD!

Have a Friendship Picnic

What You'll Need:

* A PICNIC BLANKET
* PAPER PLATES, CUPS, NAPKINS, AND PLASTIC UTENSILS
* EACH FRIEND BRINGS A PART OF THE MEAL, AND ALL FOOD SHOULD BE EASY-TO-EAT AND MAKE TREATS (CHIPS, FRUIT, SANDWICHES, SODA, COOKIES, ETC.)
* A FRISBEE, BALL, OR OUTDOOR GAME

Invite your friends to meet in the park for a picnic. It's an easy get-together that you can arrange in a snap. Beforehand, assign everyone a part of the picnic to bring (food, blanket, etc.), and then meet up in your favorite park, playground, or picnic spot. Once your blanket is laid out and the food distributed, hang out, chow down, gossip, and toss the Frisbee around. What a great way to spend a gorgeous day.

Host a Weenie Roast

What You'll Need:

* USE OF THE BACKYARD
* AN ADULT TO WORK THE BARBECUE
* POINTY WOODEN STICKS
* HOT DOGS, WITH BUNS AND TOPPINGS
  (KETCHUP, MUSTARD, RELISH, SAUERKRAUT, ETC.)
* MARSHMALLOWS
* S'MORE FIXIN'S

Can life be complete without attending at least one weenie roast? The cardinal rule of the weenie roast is as follows: If you can't cook it on a stick, it ain't on the menu.

Ask your favorite grownup to serve as chef by handling the barbecue, and have your buds bring their sense of humor. Make a night out of it—after you've digested your hot dogs, marshmallows, and S'mores (see below), tell ghost stories! If you don't know any scary stories, check out Alvin Schwartz's books *Scary Stories to Tell in the Dark*, *More Scary Stories to Tell in the Dark*, and *Scary Stories 3: More Tales to Chill Your Bones* for tales that are sure to frighten you and your friends.

GOOD OLD-FASHIONED S'MORES

What You'll Need (for 6 eaters):

* 6 STICKS (FOR TOASTING THE MARSHMALLOWS)
* 12 GRAHAM CRACKERS
* 6 HERSHEY BARS, EACH BROKEN IN TWO EQUAL PIECES
* 12 MARSHMALLOWS

What You Do:

Pop two marshmallows on each stick. Toast the marshmallows over the still-hot barbeque to crispy gooey perfection. Build your S'more by putting half of a chocolate bar onto one graham cracker. Then plop a marshmallow on top and add the other half of the chocolate bar and another graham cracker. The heat of the marshmallow between the halves of the chocolate bar will melt the chocolate a bit.

S'MORES SUNDAES!

No open fire to toast those marshmallows? No problem! This ice cream treat is based on the classic combination of marshmallows, graham crackers, and chocolate.

What You'll Need (for 6 eaters):

* ❊ 1/2 CUP OF WATER
* ❊ 1/2 CUP OF SUGAR
* ❊ 3 CUPS OF MINIATURE MARSHMALLOWS
* ❊ 3/4 TEASPOON OF VANILLA EXTRACT
* ❊ 4 OZ. SEMISWEET CHOCOLATE CHIPS
* ❊ 1/2 CUP OF WHIPPING CREAM
* ❊ 3 TABLESPOONS OF UNSALTED BUTTER
* ❊ CHOCOLATE OR VANILLA ICE CREAM, SOFTENED
* ❊ 6 GRAHAM CRACKERS, BROKEN INTO SMALL PIECES
* ❊ A MEDIUM SAUCEPAN, A SMALL SAUCEPAN, A WOODEN SPOON, 6 BOWLS, 6 SERVING SPOONS
* ❊ AN ADULT TO HELP

What You Do:

Stir the water and sugar in a medium saucepan over medium-low heat until the sugar dissolves. Simmer about 5 minutes. Turn the heat down to very low. Add 3 cups of miniature marshmallows, and stir until the marshmallows melt and the sauce is smooth. Mix in 1/4 teaspoon of vanilla extract.

Now, for the warm chocolate sauce, stir the chocolate chips, whipping cream, and butter in a small saucepan over low heat until the chocolate melts and the sauce is smooth. Mix in the remaining 1/2 teaspoon of vanilla. (Sauces can be prepared a day ahead of time. Cover separately and chill. Warm over low heat before using.)

To serve, place two scoops of ice cream in each of six bowls. Spoon the warm chocolate and marshmallow sauces over the ice cream. Top each sundae with crumbled graham crackers.

Make a Snow Sculpture

What You'll Need:

* A DRAWING OF WHAT YOU WANT TO SCULPT
* A TON OF SNOW ON THE GROUND (LIKE OVER A FOOT)
* OLD WOODEN BOARDS OR STURDY CARDBOARD PIECES
* BELOW-FREEZING TEMPS FOR A FEW DAYS IN A ROW BEFORE YOU START, AND AFTER YOU FINISH
* LARGE SPRAY BOTTLE FILLED WITH WATER

Snow sculpture is an advanced form of good old-fashioned snowman-making. The main differences are the length of time your creation can last before starting to melt, plus the extra detail you can show with your creation.

Here's How:

* Sketch what you want to sculpt first. What about an animal, like a dog, cat, or bear?

* Make a mini-mountain of snow. Prop up the sides of your mountain using the wooden boards or cardboard. Now jump up and down on the mountain to pack the snow down solid. Add more snow to the top of your pile. Repeat this again and again until you have a snow mountain at least as tall as you are. (It could take a while!)

* Sculpt your creation with your hands, like you'd make a snowman. You may want to consider using some extra tools to help you, like a sand shovel or a stick for carving.

* Accessorize! Add extra details to your sculpture using your surroundings. Pick up stones, leaves, sticks, or acorns for some extra décor.

* Spray your finished sculpture with water from the spray bottle. This frozen coating will bring out the neat, special details you've put into your creation.

Start a Book Club

What You'll Need:

❋ **A BUNCH OF GOOD BOOKS**

Book clubs are a really fun way to hang out with a cool group, and expand your literary horizons at the same time. So why not start your own?

Begin by sending an e-mail to your friends, telling them that you're starting a book club. Include the date, time, and location of your intended first meeting—either at school or at your house.

At your first meeting, discuss what types of books everybody is interested in reading. Do you have a lot of fiction fans in your crowd? A large number of history buffs? Open up the floor for ideas on a specific first title. Make sure the book your group settles on is readily available at the bookstore or at the library, is inexpensive (paperbacks are best), and that it's approved by a vote. Ask everybody to get through a few chapters a week.

Also, ask others to volunteer to host future meetings and to bring cookies and drinks. That way no one person has to be the host or the party planner the whole time.

When you meet again to discuss a few chapters, you, as your group's leader, might want to get the ball rolling by expressing your thoughts. Then open up the floor to everybody. Once all the chapters are read, it's on to book number two!

Chapter 6

BFF Fun Stuff

She's your pal. Your compadre. Your friend-to-the-end. But, shoot, even when the two of you are hanging out together, sometimes it's a snore. No longer! Get together with your closest pal, and celebrate your friendship in a big way...and this stuff can be done any ol' day!

The BFF Makeover

What You'll Need:
* YOUR BFF'S CLOSET

Next time you're hanging out at your BFF's house, and you're both looking for something to do, head into your BFF's room, and look through her closet. Challenge yourself to put together a complete outfit that you think your BFF would look great in!

The ground rules: The outfit you assemble must be a completely original combo—nothing she's worn together before. Include not just a top and a bottom, but barrettes, earrings, a choker, shoes—the whole shebang!

Have your BFF model your selection, and make adjustments—change up the belt, or tweak the collar of her shirt in a different direction. Do a full hairdo on your BFF, too! REALLY fun. Then when you are done with that, switch!

Role Reversal

What You'll Need:
* A FREE RUN OF EACH OTHER'S CLOSETS

Here's a nutty little piece of wool to pull over your whole crew's eyes. Go over to your BFF's house, and dress up as her from head to toe. Put on one of her fave outfits (one that all your buds would recognize as hers—if you guys aren't close in size, look for stuff in your closet that resembles her stuff and add her favorite earrings, necklace, whatever, to drive the point home). Then do your hair and stuff the way that she always does.

Now, you two should bop on over to your house, and she should deck herself out in your exact image. Lend her your most identifiable style tips. Then meet up with your other friends or family members and look surprised when they can't quite figure out what's different about you two.

Create a BFF Crossword Puzzle

What You'll Need:

* ❋ A CROSSWORD PUZZLE TO USE AS A MODEL
* ❋ BLANK PAPER
* ❋ A PEN
* ❋ A RULER TO MAKE CROSSWORD PUZZLE SQUARES

Does your BFF really know what makes you tick? Test her knowledge by making up a crossword puzzle about yourself. Write clues based on your likes and dislikes—for example, four across might be, "The only movie that ever made me cry." The answer, *Titanic*, is spelled out in squares.

To make the crossword puzzle itself, count up the number of letters in each of your word answers, and make a box for each letter, using a ruler to keep your boxes straight. Use any crossword puzzle from the newspaper as your how-to sample. Coordinate the across and down answers so they overlap.

Set Off Sparks in the Dark

Just for Fun

Urban legend has it that chewing Wint-o-green Life Savers quickly will actually set off little white-green sparks you can see in the dark. Guess what? This rumor's actually true. We've done it! We've seen it! It's coooooool.

Try it yourself. Head into a pitch-dark room or closet. Toss about five minty little friends into your mouth, and start chewing immediately, as fast as you can. Part your lips slightly—see sparks shooting out? It might take a little practice, but you'll get the hang of it. All your buds can give this trick a try—you could actually chew in pairs, and spot the sparkin' simultaneously.

Send an Invisible Note

What You'll Need:

* WHITE PAPER
* A PAINTBRUSH
* LEMON JUICE
* WATER
* A HAIRDRYER (FOR YOUR BFF)

Got a secret that you want only your BFF to know? Get sneaky and tell her in a letter written with invisible ink!

Take a sheet of white paper and use a paintbrush dipped in diluted lemon juice (that means you need to add a little bit of water to the juice) to pen your note. Then let it dry. Make sure your BFF knows what to do when she gets the letter, or she'll think you just slipped her a blank sheet.

Read the secret note by blowing hot air from a hairdryer over the sheet of paper. In a short time, she'll see what you wrote as it turns brown on the page! If you want, offer to give her what's left of your invisible ink—she'll probably want to write you something *juicy* back!

Play *What If* with Your Friends

Just for Fun

Make up questions for each other, i.e., what if you won a million dollars but you couldn't keep it. Who would you give it to and why?

Say Cheese!

What You'll Need:

* A COUPLE OF DOLLARS
* A WILD-AND-CRAZY 'TUDE

Grab your BFF and head for the nearest instant photo-booth at the mall, amusement park, or arcade. Cram into the booth, get goofy, and say, "Cheese!"

Long Time, No Talk?
Send a Faraway Friend a Taped Message

What You'll Need:

* ❋ A DICTAPHONE OR SMALL TAPE RECORDER
* ❋ AUDIO TAPE

Instead of writing to your far-off friend, send her a tape. You can say all you want to say without tiring your typing fingers or writing your wrist off. She'll love hearing your voice, and even more so than writing her, you might actually feel like you're talking to her! Making your tape can be ongoing. You can take it to school and have guest voice appearances from mutual friends. You can also put some of her favorite tunes on low in the background and chat away!

Then Hey, Why Not Make Her a Video Diary!

What You'll Need:

* ❋ A CAMCORDER AND A BLANK CASSETTE
* ❋ A LITTLE IMAGINATION

If you've got a faraway BFF, why not make a cool video diary? Grab the family camcorder, think like a movie director, and capture special moments on tape!

* ❀ If your BFF moved away from your neighborhood, conduct interviews with old friends and neighbors.
* ❀ Take a walking tour of your town and your old haunts.
* ❀ Hang out in your room and gossip to the camera, just as if she were with you.
* ❀ Video friends at the softball game, or capture some great party moments on tape so she can see her old pals. She'll be so touched!

Another cool idea along these lines: Photograph your old neighborhood for a future flashback. Years from now, recalling memories in perfect detail can get difficult. Ensure a future nostalgia rush by taking pics of your crib, your friends and family, the stop sign at the end of your block—the world you live in. She'll love it...and so will you!

Who's the best BFF in the world? That'd be you, sister! Here are a few groovy ideas of stuff you can do for your BFF to make her feel special.

THE BFF BIRTHDAY BOOK

What You'll Need:

* ✳ A BLANK JOURNAL BOOK OR SCRAPBOOK
* ✳ PHOTOS OF YOUR BUD
* ✳ MEMORABILIA OF ALL THE GOOD TIMES YOU'VE HAD TOGETHER

Celebrate your BFF's special day by making her a birthday book! Here are some great ideas to get you going:

❀ Write a mini-history about your friend, her family, her hobbies, and her hopes and dreams. Include the details of how and when you met. Jot down your first impression of her and the moment you knew she was the real deal.

❀ Collect mega-compliments about her from her other buds and family, and quote them.

❀ With photo-safe tabs, adhere photos, concert tickets, notes, and all the good stuff you've treasured through your friendship. Include the what-when-where-and-who details next to the memorabilia so she'll remember it all forever.

❀ Decorate the pages with borders and cute titles.

"GOOD-FOR-ONE" BFF COUPONS

What You'll Need:

* ✳ CONSTRUCTION PAPER
* ✳ SCISSORS
* ✳ MAGIC MARKERS
* ✳ STICKERS, GLITTER, STAMPS, RIBBON, OR ANYTHING ELSE YOU CAN THINK OF TO DECORATE AND MAKE YOUR GIFT SPECIAL (OPTIONAL)

Next time you have trouble coming up with a gift for your BFF, why not create adorable IOU gift coupons? You can make her little booklets out of construction paper that include "good-for-one"

B.F.F. Coupons

gift cards with all things that are meaningful to her! Here are some ideas to get you started:

❀ Good for one free banana split (yep, I'm buying!)

❀ Good for one math tutoring session (so she aces her algebra test)

❀ Good for one night of eating popcorn and watching her favorite movies

Catch Fireflies in a Jar

What You'll Need:

❋ A LARGE, CLEAR WIDE-MOUTHED JAR WITH A LID, WITH SMALL HOLES POKED IN THE LID WITH A PENCIL

If you've never tried to catch fireflies in a jar before, it's a summer night treat that can't be beat. Go outside a little after dusk, which is the social hour in most bug circles. As it starts to get dark, look in your backyard or nearby woods, and you'll see those little bright fellas buzzing around. The fun of catching a firefly is to chase it, so start running around like a goofball, holding your jar wide open. Don't use candy or sugar to bait the bugs—use your wits and speed only!

When you finally catch a bug, screw your jar shut as fast as you can. Watch your firefly dart and zap around inside, with its bright light sparking everywhere. Enjoy the view—then respect the firefly's rights (make sure not to keep 'em too long, since there can't be much air in that jar), and let the little guy go free.

Chapter 7

Money Makers

Think you're too young to make a buck? Think again. In fact, you can even start your own business—and appoint yourself president. Be your only employee (that means more work, but less people to split your profit with), or enlist the help of some biz-minded buddies. Your piggy bank will thank you either way—and you'll have loads of fun learning how to earn a dollar. Cha-ching!

Start a Purple Punch Stand

What You'll Need:

* ✳ SEEDLESS GRAPES
* ✳ SEVERAL LARGE PITCHERS
* ✳ POSTER BOARD AND FAT PURPLE MARKERS OR PENS FOR MAKING PURPLE PUNCH POSTERS
* ✳ SEVERAL CANS OF GRAPE JUICE CONCENTRATE
* ✳ SEVERAL LITERS OF GINGER ALE
* ✳ A BIG WOODEN MIXING SPOON
* ✳ A BIG BAG OF ICE CUBES (OR AN OVER-ACTIVE ICE MAKER)
* ✳ A COOLER AND SOME FREEZER PACKS
* ✳ A SMALL PORTABLE TABLE AND A FEW CHAIRS
* ✳ PLASTIC CUPS (OF COURSE, PURPLE IS PREFERABLE)
* ✳ SUNSCREEN, SHADES, AN EMPTY SHOE BOX, AND A BOOM BOX!

It's sticky, stifling, and hot outside. What's a girl to do? Hey! Put a twist on an old favorite! What screams summer louder than an impromptu lemonade stand? Get off that sofa and brave the boiling temps—passers-by will be psyched for a fresh and fruity homemade thirst quencher! And your wallet won't object to a little sweetening up, either! But instead of mixing up cups of grocery store lemonade concentrate, be the first girl on the block to open a Purple Punch stand!

❀ The night before you open up shop, stick a couple bunches of seedless grapes in the freezer.

❀ In the morning, invite your neighborhood buds to get in on the action. Ask 'em to bring over a couple of clean pitchers, too. Make signs and post 'em around the neighborhood advertising your super-sweet deal. How does a quarter per cup sound?

❀ Make several pitchers of grape juice from concentrate by following the directions on the label. Then split the juice among several more pitchers, making sure each one is only half full. Fill the rest with ginger ale, leaving enough room for ice cubes. Stir. Add the ice and stir again.

- ❀ Fill a cooler with sealable bags of ice and cold freezer packs. Don't forget to bag and pack up the frozen grapes from the night before!
- ❀ Before filling cups for customers, toss in a couple of frozen grapes. Then pour in the sparkling grape juice. Mmm!

TIP: Make sure you have enough change in your register (shoe box) before your first customer stops by.

Start a Dog-Walking Biz

SOLO OR WITH A BUD

What You'll Need:
- ✳ SOME OF THE ANTSY PUPS FROM YOUR NEIGHBORHOOD
- ✳ A SELECTION OF LEASHES
- ✳ DOGGIE TREATS

Are you an animal lover who wants to make extra cash? Then start a dog-walking business! No doubt there are lonely pups on your block whose owners have to work long hours. Knock on doors and offer to give your neighbors' pets a much-needed shot of sunshine, fresh air, and exercise every afternoon!

A few tips to keep in mind: A fair fee to charge is about $10 per dog per week—and hey, if you walk more than one dog, the green can really add up! In order to truly earn your keep, though, you've got to stay on your toes. Walk the dogs five times a week, Monday through Friday. Pick up the pups as soon as school lets out—and don't forget! Make sure you get any and all special instructions and contact info (in case of emergency) from each dog's owner right from the start. And if you *do* end up walking more than one dog at once, just observe common sense: Make sure you don't walk so many at the same time that you're overwhelmed, and make sure that the dogs get along with each other. (In other words, try not to mix pit bulls with poodles.)

Have a Garage Sale

What You'll Need:

* ❊ EVERYTHING IN YOUR CLOSET YOU HAVEN'T WORN IN A YEAR
* ❊ KNICK-KNACKS, STUFFED ANIMALS, TOYS WITH NO SENTIMENTAL VALUE
* ❊ STUFF YOUR PARENTS DON'T NEED ANY MORE
* ❊ TABLE AND BENCHES/CHAIRS
* ❊ CARDBOARD, MASKING TAPE, AND MARKERS

Look around your room. How many old toys are on the shelves or under the bed that you'll simply never play with again because— hello?—you're not six years old anymore? And check out the garage. If you cleaned it, you'd probably find tons of things your folks would rather sell than keep and junk up their storage space. Time to get organized and sell all the "worthless" loot in a garage sale!

First, go through your closet. Put clothes in a pile that aren't somewhat in style or classic. Same goes for shoes, belts, hats, and accessories. They may seem junky to you, but they probably won't be to someone at your sale. Next, survey your room. Do you *really* need a pink bunny that now has a stain? Someone might buy that as a dog's toy, and then you're up a dollar!

Now, go to your folks and tell them your plan. Ask them if you can clean out the garage (guess what the answer will be?!). It's likely that they'll tell you which boxes are probably junk, and which ones they don't want you price-tagging.

Organize everything by categories: shirts, pants, knick-knacks, miscellaneous, and so on. Ask for a parental inspection so you don't accidentally sell something they want to keep. Using the cardboard and markers, make signs announcing your sale (include your address—provide directions if needed—and the date and time of the sale). Tape your signs around neighborhood street poles. Set your alarm and hit the sack—successful garage sales start early.

On the day of the sale, wear an outfit with good pockets. If you have boxes to put categorized stuff into, do that. Hang as many clothes as you can on fence edges, bushes, and/or the top of the garage door. Take the masking tape and write a price for each item, then rip off the ready-made price-tag and stick it to the item. People (like to have to ask, "How much is this?" Price things cheap. Believe not, even 25 cents here and there adds up.

HINT: If a friend wants to join you with her unwanted loot, be sure and keep her stuff separate from yours.

When the sale is over, pack up and ask your mom to take you and the leftover stuff to a charity drop-off. Also, count the money you made. It could be a lot, it might be a little—but you'll have uncluttered your closet, your room, and the garage, talked to a lot of passers-by, and made a little dough.

NOTE: People might "haggle" you, which means they'll try to talk you down from your marked price for something. Be flexible. Don't forget that this is all stuff you would probably give to Goodwill, or the Salvation Army, or throw away, anyway. Be friendly, and keep aware as people show up.

Be a Party Assistant

What You'll Need:
❋ **A FESTIVE ATTITUDE**

Do you have a knack for entertaining little kids? Share your talent by offering to help out at neighborhood kiddie birthday parties— for cash! You can assist the adults in leading games, making balloon animals, face-painting, and starting sing-alongs. Grateful parents are likely to pay you to keep the kids busy! You could even enlist a friend or two to help with big bashes.

Chapter 8

Munchy Madness

Tummy growling? Put away the PB&J. It's time to give your palate a taste of something new. Here's some fresh food for thought— from exotic fruits to newfangled grilled cheese, from easy-to-make pizza to subs. *Still* thinking about that PB&J? Whip up a jar of home-made peanut butter! Get cookin' and get munchin'.

The Tallest Sandwich in the World

What You'll Need:

* **MEGA SANDWICH FIXIN'S** (VARIOUS COLD CUTS, VEGGIES LIKE LETTUCE AND TOMATO, BREAD OR ROLLS, AND VARIOUS TOPPINGS LIKE MAYO, MUSTARD, SALAD DRESSINGS, BARBEQUE SAUCE, SALT AND PEPPER)

Invite the gang over for a truly important test of skill and will: To see who can build the tallest sub known to humankind. Ask everybody to pitch in by bringing bread, deli meats (turkey, roast beef, ham), veggies, cheese, what have you.

The rules of the game: Everybody gets five minutes to build. All sandwich architects start and finish at the same time. And no matter whose sandwich ends up being the highest, everyone's a winner— the whole gang gets to eat the end results!

Top This! Make-Your-Own Pizza

What You'll Need:

* **1 PACKAGE OF YEAST**
* **WATER**
* **1 TEASPOON OF SUGAR**
* **2-3/4 CUPS OF FLOUR**
* **2 TABLESPOON OF OLIVE OIL**
* **1 TEASPOON OF SALT**
* **STUFF FOR SAUCE** (SEE NEXT PAGE)
* **YOUR FAVORITE CHEESE** (SHREDDED) **AND TOPPINGS** (LIKE MUSHROOMS, PEPPERONI SLICES, CHOPPED PEPPERS, ETC.)
* **OLIVE OIL COOKING SPRAY**
* **A SMALL BOWL, 2 LARGE BOWLS, MEASURING CUPS AND MEASURING SPOONS, A WHISK, A PIZZA PAN OR COOKIE SHEET**
* **PLASTIC WRAP AND A DISH TOWEL**

Sure you could order pizza or even use pre-made pizza dough you can get at the store. But did you ever try making your own pizza?

It's easier than you think and tons of fun to make with friends! This recipe is for two pizzas, enough to keep the whole gang munching.

1. In a small bowl, dissolve the yeast in 1/2 cup of warm water. Then add the sugar. When this combo has foamed up, put it in a large bowl with 2 cups of the flour, 1 cup of warm water, the oil, and the salt. Whisk the ingredients until everything is well mixed. Add more flour, a bit at a time, until the dough holds together.

2. Turn out the dough onto a floured surface. Knead it until it's smooth. Coat the inside of another large bowl with olive oil cooking spray, and put the kneaded ball of dough into the bowl. Roll the ball around to coat it with oil. Cover the dough with plastic wrap and put it into a turned-off oven to rise for about 30 minutes. As you wait for the dough to rise, it's a good time to start making the sauce.

3. When the dough has doubled in size, push it down and divide it into two balls. Cover one with a dish towel while you roll the other into a 12- to 14-inch circle. Fold in the edges to form the crust of your pizza. Place on a pizza pan or cookie sheet, then spread the sauce out, add your favorite toppings (like pepperoni, onions, and/or green peppers) and finally top with cheese (mozzarella is classic). Let your topped pizza rest for a bit while you roll out the second ball of dough and preheat the oven to 475 degrees. Once your second pizza is ready and the oven is preheated, bake both pies for 15 to 20 minutes, or until the crusts are golden.

SUPER EASY PIZZA SAUCE

What You'll Need:

* 1 TABLESPOON OF OLIVE OIL
* 1 DICED ONION
* 1 MINCED GARLIC CLOVE
* 2 TEASPOONS OF DRIED OREGANO
* 1 15-OZ. CAN OF TOMATO SAUCE
* 1 6-OZ. CAN OF TOMATO PASTE
* A SKILLET AND A WOODEN SPOON
* AN ADULT TO HELP

Sure you can buy pizza sauce in a jar but this is way cheaper and yummier.

In a skillet, have a adult help heat the oil and sauté the onion, garlic, and oregano for 5 minutes. Add the tomato sauce and tomato paste, and simmer, uncovered, for another 10 minutes. Stir occasionally to make sure that the sauce doesn't burn. Makes enough for 2 pizzas.

Give New Life to Grilled Cheese

What You'll Need:

* YOUR FAVORITE BREAD (2 SLICES)
* CHEDDAR CHEESE
* TOMATOES
* RED ONIONS
* MELTED BUTTER
* A NONSTICK PAN, A COOKING BRUSH (FOR THE MELTED BUTTER), AND A SPATULA
* AN ADULT TO HELP YOU USE THE STOVETOP

Cheerio! Next time you make a toasty grilled cheese for lunch, why not prepare it the way they do in England? Take a slice of bread and then add a slice of cheddar, a thin slice of ripe tomato, and thinly sliced red onion. Slap on another slice of cheddar, and add another slice of bread on top. Brush the outside of each slice of bread with melted butter. Then grill in a heated nonstick pan (add a little more melted butter if necessary) over low heat until the sandwich is well-toasted and melty. *Right then!*

P.S. Want to switch it up even more? Try substituting some sliced green apple for the tomatoes and red onions. Cheddar cheese and apples taste great together!

Make Your Own Peanut Butter

What You'll Need:

* 1-1/2 CUPS OF UNSALTED ROASTED PEANUTS (YOU CAN TRY ALMONDS OR CASHEWS, TOO)
* 1 TABLESPOON OF PEANUT OR CANOLA OIL
* A FOOD PROCESSOR OR BLENDER
* A BUTTER KNIFE OR SPOON (DEPENDING ON WHAT YOU'RE GOING TO USE YOUR PB FOR)

So cinchy and delish. Do-it-yourself, and get ready for a very satisfying snack!

Simply place the peanuts and oil into a food processor or blender, and blend until smooth. If you prefer chunky peanut butter, save about a half-cup of the peanuts to add at the end. Pulse (in a food processor or blender) for a few seconds, just enough to break up the peanuts.

Yummy Serving Suggestions:

- ✿ Spread homemade PB on an apple or English muffin
- ✿ Mix into plain yogurt
- ✿ Swirl into a smoothie
- ✿ Spread onto a piece of chocolate for a do-it-yourself candy rush!

P.S. You can make other kinds of nut butters, too. Try almond butter or cashew butter.

Make Fruit-Filled Ice Cubes

SOLO OR WITH A GROUP OF BUDS

What You'll Need:

- ❊ AN ICE CUBE TRAY
- ❊ WATER
- ❊ TWO PIECES OF FRESH FRUIT, FINELY SLICED
  (LIKE STRAWBERRIES, LEMONS, RASPBERRIES, OR ORANGES)
- ❊ SOME FREEZER SPACE

Those expensive, fancy-flavored waters are all the rage, but why spend the bucks when you can have fun making fruit-filled ice cubes to float in and flavor water yourself? It's beyond easy!

1. Fill all of the slots in your ice cube tray with water, about halfway.

2. Place small pieces of fruit in each ice cube slot.

3. Pop the tray into the freezer and let your cubes form.

4. Plop your cubes into your drink of choice, but keep in mind once the ice melts, the fruit will be in your drink. You want to make sure it's a yummy treat. Why not try these tasty combos: Strawberry ice cubes in chocolate milk, apple chunk ice cubes in ginger ale, raspberry ice cubes in lemonade, lemon or orange chunk ice cubes in iced tea. Yummy!

Rutti, Tutti, Fresh and Fruity Exotic Edibles

What You'll Need:

❋ A RAINBOW OF FRESH FRUIT FLAVOR

❋ AN APPETITE FOR ADVENTURE

Why not branch out and try an exotic, tropical edible? Thought mangoes were just for body lotion? Guess again! There's no need to hop on a jet and sweat it out by the Equator in order to get a taste of the tropics. Actually, you probably don't have to go much farther than your local gourmet grocery store.

SOME POSSIBILITIES:

❧ **PAPAYA**: An over-grown pear-shaped fruit with a bright yellow/gold skin. They're juicy and you should expect a unique sweet and tart flavor. Inside, you'll find a whole lot of little black seeds—pass on eating those puppies.

❧ **MANGO**: Once considered sacred in India, mangoes are now grown in warm places all over. They can be a tough pick because their shapes are unpredictable. Oval, round, or kidney-shaped, they ripen to a rich, gorgeous red with gold and yellow fruit inside. They have a delicious sweet and tart taste.

❧ **POMELO**: Considered the grapefruit's long lost relative, these yellow or pinkish-brown fruits are the size of a way big mega-melon! They boast a wide range of tastes—from super-sweet to very tart and everything in between.

❧ **PASSION FRUIT**: Who could resist? Brazilian natives, these small egg-shaped fruits are deep purple on the outside and gold inside. Don't worry about their little seeds—they're perfectly edible.

❧ **STAR FRUIT**: Way cool! These shiny, waxy, yellowish fruits are divided into five sections. So, when you slice them horizontally, the pieces look like...stars!

❧ **GUAVA**: These South American natives can range from egg-size to the size of a large orange, and they can span the rainbow—if they're green, let them fully ripen.

Make Your Own Snow Cones Just for (Winter) Fun

What You'll Need:

* A MIXING BOWL
* WOODEN SPOON OR CLEAN SAND SHOVEL
* SNOW ON THE GROUND
* PLASTIC OR PAPER CUPS, PREFERABLY MINI ONES, BUT REGULAR SIZE WILL DO
* TOPPINGS: MAPLE SYRUP, KOOL-AID, FRUIT JUICE, OR YOUR FAVE SODA
* PLASTIC WRAP
* YOUR FREEZER

Steaming drinks aren't the only tasty thirst-quenchers to enjoy during the winter. Ever thought of having a snow cone after an afternoon of outdoor fun? You may as well take advantage of all the white fluff out there. And, snow cones are delicious! So try making 'em yourself the natural, easy way—and enjoy a chilly outdoor treat while you're in the warm indoors.

1. Head out into the backyard and scoop some clean snow into a mixing bowl. The best kind of snow to use is frozen-over with a little ice—not fresh-fallen flakes.

2. Head inside and scoop snow into each of your cups. Make as many as you want.

3. Now, pour the topping of your choice over the snow in each cup. The topping will seep through your snow, spreading the flavor throughout.

4. Chomp away immediately, or cover each cup with plastic wrap and pop in the freezer for later.

Make "Edible Eyeballs"

What You'll Need:
* ❋ A BUNCH OF GRAPES
* ❋ YOUR FREEZER

Edible eyeballs sound stomach-turning, but they're not! Pop a bunch of grapes into the freezer for half an hour, then take them out. They won't be frozen stiff, just firm, yet a little squishy—like little eyeballs! Avoid dwelling on the similarities for too long by gobbling 'em up— and enjoying them—right away.

Smooth Operator: DIY Smoothies

What You'll Need:
* ❋ A BLENDER
* ❋ 1 CUP OF FRUIT (TRY A COMBO LIKE STRAWBERRIES/BANANAS/ SHREDDED COCONUT, OR RASPBERRIES/BLUEBERRIES/ STRAWBERRIES, OR PINEAPPLES/ORANGES/BANANAS)
* ❋ 1-1/2 CUPS OF MILK
* ❋ 2 TEASPOONS OF HONEY
* ❋ COUPLE OF ICE CUBES
* ❋ 2 TALL GLASSES

Quench your thirst with this frothy health shake. Simply dump all of the ingredients into your blender and let it whirl. Blend until the mixture is smooth. Serve immediately. Makes two tall glasses.

Chapter 9

She's Crafty

Bring out the budding artist in you. Even if you're artistically challenged, anybody can do these simple craft how-to's. And there's no need to drop a ton of cash at the supplies store either. All these projects can be completed for cheap.

Fringe Benefits: Dress Up Your Denim

What You'll Need:
* ❋ A PAIR OF OLD JEANS
* ❋ A PAIR OF SCISSORS

Up your denim's cool factor! Almost instantly you can turn your old castaway denim into chic and trendy jeans! Or, if you're constantly tripping over too-long jeans, just cut them at the hems. Not only will they fit better, they'll look even cooler!

How To:

1. Carefully cut off the hems of both legs.
2. Cut the seam along the top of the waistband (the lower you cut, the lower they'll be—so, try on your jeans first and make a mark where you plan to cut).
3. Throw the jeans in the washer and dryer. Trim any super-long strings and—*bam!* Fabulously fringed low-riders!

P.S. You can fringe jean skirts and jean jackets, too (cut along cuffs, collar, and/or waistband).

Hats Off! Update an Old Hat

What You'll Need:
* ❋ A BASEBALL HAT
* ❋ BUTTONS, PINS, AND FLASHY PIERCED EARRINGS

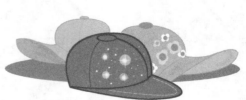

Plunge into your old jewelry box for sparkly earrings or gaudy pins you used to play dress-up with. Comb through dresser drawers for pins or buttons with cool sayings and unusually shaped decorative pins. Most craft stores have buttons and beads and all sorts of baubles. Or, plan ahead and search rummage sales and Goodwill shops for unique goodies for cheap! Arrange jewels until your cap looks as fancy as a crown. You'll rule!

DIY Beaded Earrings

What You'll Need:

* ✲ A PAIR OF HOOP EARRINGS
* ✲ SMALL, LIGHTWEIGHT COLORED BEADS WITH PRE-MADE HOLES
  (AVAILABLE AT ANY CRAFT STORE)

Looking for the perfect earrings to pair with your peasant tops and frayed, faded jeans? Homemade, beaded hoops fit the bill. Don't have pierced ears? Pin a group of earrings onto your jean jacket for a supercool look.

Here's How:

1. Unclasp the hoop earrings.
2. Choose a bead and slide it onto a hoop.
3. Continue sliding beads onto the earring until the hoop is covered.
4. Repeat steps 1–3 with the other earring. (You can make the same pattern or a different one!)

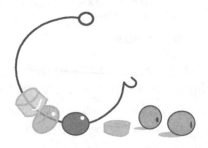

Try on your new hippie-hoops! Groovy, baby.

Paint Some Life Into a Plain T-shirt

What You'll Need:

* ✲ A PLAIN WHITE T
* ✲ FABRIC-SAFE PAINTS FROM A CRAFT STORE

Spruce up a plain-old tee with fabric paint. Go nuts—stripes, polka dots, something all artsy and abstract, your favorite quote, or whatever strikes your fancy!

Try Tie Dye

What You'll Need:

* ✳ A WARM, SUNNY DAY SO YOU CAN DYE OUTSIDE
* ✳ NEWSPAPER OR PAINTER'S DROP CLOTH, PAPER TOWELS, AND GARBAGE BAGS
* ✳ RUBBER GLOVES
* ✳ CLEAN WHITE OR LIGHT-COLORED TANKS, TEES, BOXERS, PILLOWCASES, ETC.
* ✳ RUBBER BANDS
* ✳ ONE BUCKET FOR EACH COLOR OF DYE
  (THAT HOLDS ABOUT 4 GALLONS EACH)
* ✳ PERMANENT FABRIC DYE
* ✳ A SUPER-LONG SPOON OR GRILLING TONGS
  (FOR STIRRING THE DYE AND RETRIEVING DYED ITEMS FROM BUCKETS OF DYE)
* ✳ SCISSORS

Dying to pump some personality into tired tees or blah boxers? Can't figure out what to do with that white V-neck—the one sporting that stubborn ketchup splatter? Rather than toss it out or leave it on your closet floor hoping that by some miracle the spot will disappear, give that shirt a second chance at life! You can also pick up a multi-pack of white undershirts, tanks, or boxers at your local discount store for cheap! Or, hey, add instant funk to your room! Scrounge up a plain white sheet that's seen better days. With a couple of twists, ties, and dunks, you can transform that sheet into a one-of-a-kind wall hanging!

Here's How:

1. Head outside with all your supplies and scope a spot to set up shop, like your driveway, garage, or yard—preferably near a hose or sink for filling buckets and for accessible clean up.

2. Lay down newspaper or a drop cloth to protect grass or pavement.

3. Slip those gloves on! After all, it *is* dye...so, it dyes just about everything (including hands and nails, at least temporarily).

4. With an adult's help, follow instructions on the box of dye.

5. Lay your shirt (boxers, pillowcases, etc.) out flat on a clean, dry surface and arm yourself with a handful of rubber bands.

6. Wrap, fold, and twist random sections of your shirt (or whatever you're dyeing) with rubber bands to create all sorts of psychedelic patterns and designs. Those sections covered by the coiled rubber bands won't be dyed, and that fabric will remain its original color—in a ring shape surrounded by the dyed sections that weren't covered. Space the rubber bands far apart or really close together for added variation. (Band the front and back of your shirt and sleeves, too!)

TIP: Stick the prongs of a fork into fabric, twist the fabric in a circular direction, and band that section for a cool, spiral design.

7. Once your shirt looks nothing like its former self, it's time to dye. Remember, colors will spread, run, and overlap, and that's the whole beauty of tie-dye. But, it's best to start with the lightest color(s). *Check out instructions to see if you need to rinse your material in cold water before dipping into another color.*

8. Once you're done dyeing, snip the rubber bands, and let your fabulous fashions dry in the sun.

IMPORTANT! After dyeing and drying, wash everything SEPARATELY in COLD water! Best to do this immediately so you don't accidentally wash it with the rest of your laundry and dye everything!

Make a Funky Headband

What You'll Need:
* ❋ SCISSORS
* ❋ ABOUT 12-INCHES OF BLACK VELVET FABRIC, 2-INCHES IN WIDTH (OR ANY COLOR YOU PREFER)
* ❋ RULER
* ❋ A PLAIN PLASTIC HEADBAND
* ❋ GLUE
* ❋ RUBBER BANDS
* ❋ DECORATIVE MATERIAL (OPTIONAL)

Have a drawer full of unused hair accessories? Pull out those unused headbands—the ones that look so cool, but don't seem worth the pain. But, they don't have to hurt, you know! Here's your chance to revamp your headbands.

1. Use scissors to cut a piece of velvet measuring 12" x 2".
2. Take your plastic headband and velvet fabric in hand. Place the velvet fabric against the top of your headband, lengthwise.
3. Glue the fabric to the top of the band, wrap the ends underneath and glue them in place—when the fabric covers the teeth of your band, it rests much more gently on your head.
4. Secure each end of your headband with a rubber band to hold the fabric in place until the glue dries.
5. Let dry for at least two hours.
6. When your headband is dry, you can decide whether you want to leave it sleek and neat— *Alice in Wonderland*-style—or decorate it with gems, beads, ribbons, sequins, or anything else that suits you! If you choose to decorate your band, just use some more glue to secure the decorations, and let dry again. Then, slide the headband onto your head. Looking good!

Step 2

Step 3

Step 6

Put Your Best Foot Forward!

What You'll Need:

* YOUR SHOES AND/OR SNEAKS
* COOL COLORED LACES, RIBBONS, OR BUNGEE CORD

Who says you have to string plain old white laces through your Keds? Not us! Why not thread some bungee cord instead? Or, try gorgeous ribbons, strong yarn, friendship bracelets (only not tied off)—whatever keeps you on your toes!

Make Your Own Stencils

What You'll Need:

* CONSTRUCTION PAPER
* A PENCIL
* SCISSORS

Ever try to redraw something—a picture, shape, or design—after you've already drawn it once? It's really hard to get both drawings to look the same! That's the genius behind stencils. They'll help you maintain uniformity. They work kind of like cookie cutters, but for paper. And they're pretty simple to make, with a little imagination.

Take a piece of construction paper, whatever size you want, and use a pencil to draw the shape. Then, carefully use your pencil to poke a hole in the middle of the shape (make sure you're poking it in a spot that will eventually be cut out). Starting at this hole, use scissors to carefully cut out the shape you drew.

Now you have a stencil. Trace it several times to make a border around some paper—suddenly you have personal stationery! Make several stencils and create your own pictures with them. Overlap the shapes as you trace, or flip your stencil so it's facing the other direction, just to shake things up a bit. And when you draw something you really like, use your stencils to create it again—it should be much simpler the next time around!

Photo Mobile

Solo

What You'll Need:

- **A handful of your favorite photos**
- **Clear-drying craft glue**
- **Colored poster board**
- **Scissors**
- **1–2 wire coat hangers**
- **Transparent fishing line**
- **Colorful ribbon or yard** (about 1 yard)
- **All sorts of beads** (the ones used for jewelry making)
- **A one-hole hole puncher**

A photo mobile is a cool way to display your favorite photos—frame-free!

1. Select some must-hang pictures. Glue pieces of colored poster board onto the back of each photo so you won't see the camera-paper side of your pics as they twirl on your mobile. Leave extra colored poster board around your picture if you want a border.
2. Let the glue dry. Then, cut out pictures in different shapes and sizes. Try tracing things, like soup cans, for a perfect circle shape. Or just cut some shapes freehand.
3. If you're using two coat hangers, hang the second coat hanger on the first and secure it tightly with fishing line. For added security, add blobs of clear drying glue to both sides of the secured hanger's "neck."
4. Feel like decorating more? Cover the necks and sides of your hangers with ribbon or yarn. Use two colors of yarn, knot them around the neck of your hanger and twist together, one over the other down and

along your hanger. Also, it's easier if you cover the sides first. Glue on decorative beads, too.

5. Set your hanger(s) flat on the floor and place your pictures where you'd like them to hang. By using different lengths of fishing line or yarn, you can adjust where your pictures will hang.

6. With pictures in place, punch holes in each one where you want it to hang from (upside down, sideways, etc.).

7. Measure lengths of fishing line accordingly to hang photos at the lengths you chose. Cut each piece individually. Thread each piece of line through the punched hole, and knot. Then, tie the other to its designated spot on the hanger. Add a dab of clear-drying glue to either side of the knots on your hanger to keep lines in place as you go along. Continue until the hanger is to your liking. Secure the fishing line around the neck of the hanger and hang the mobile with the other end!

Glam Up Fashion Magazines

SOLO

What You'll Need:
* ❋ FASHION MAGS
* ❋ SCISSORS
* ❋ FINE-POINT MAGIC MARKERS

Ever page through one of your mom's or older sister's superchic fashion mags to check out the clothing spreads? Gorgeous models clad in elegant clothes everywhere you look? But wait—that chick wearing the sparkling silvery floor-length number is missing something—but what?

Cut out the most glam fashion pictures you can find, then use your big beautiful imagination and go to town! Draw additions to improve the outfits (handbags, shoes, jewelry—you get the drift). Fun on *loooooooong* car trips.

Pressed for Time

What You'll Need:

* ❋ **LEAVES OR FLOWERS**
* ❋ **WAXED PAPER**
* ❋ **A SUPER-BIG, HARDCOVER BOOK**
  (LIKE A DICTIONARY. IF YOU HAVE SEVERAL BIG BOOKS, THAT'S EVEN BETTER!)
* ❋ **TWEEZERS** (OPTIONAL)

Next time you take a fab vacation or visit out-of-town friends or relatives, take home a keepsake, for free! By pressing super-pretty or sentimental leaves or flowers, you can preserve a special memory. Or use a variety of flowers and leaves for all sorts of crafty projects.

1. Gather an assortment of big, bright, flawless leaves and flowers. Fiery fall leaves and colorful flat flowers like pansies and daisies are ideal!

2. Make sure to completely dry the flowers and leaves.

3. If you have a flower press, that's fab! Otherwise, place each leaf or flower between two pieces of waxed paper and stick each one between separate pages of your book, towards the book's spine. For extra insurance, stack several heavy books on top. You can mark the outside of the pages where your flowers are, with slips of paper so it'll be easier to find them.

4. Allow them to stay, untouched, for about a week to ten days.

5. When it's time, slowly open your book and you should find beautifully pressed flowers and leaves. They are fragile, so remove carefully—tweezers work best.

6. Now what? It's up to you! Here are a couple of ideas to spark your imagination:

   ❀ If you pressed keepsakes from a special time and place, add them to your scrapbook. For protection, leave them in the waxed paper and just trim it down to size. Adhere to your album or memory book.

   ❀ Add a flower to nice, heavy-stock paper with craft glue to create one-of-a-kind invites or notecards.

✿ Using two pieces of sturdy, transparent contact paper, make placemats. Simply peel the back off a piece of contact paper and place your flowers and leaves on the sticky side in a design or pattern. Then, peel the backing off another piece of contact paper and carefully lay it on top. Press them together until the two pieces of contact paper are stuck together strongly. Trim, if necessary.

Make a Daisy Chain — Just for (Summer) Fun

What You'll Need:

* AN ABUNDANCE OF DAISIES
* A LITTLE SUNSHINE

Next time you pick a daisy, don't rush to pull off the petals and chant *loves me* and *loves me nots*! Instead, carefully pluck a flower at the base of its stem, as close to the ground as you can get. Pick a bunch. When you've got your hands full of flowers, make a daisy chain.

1. Pick up two flowers and tie the stem in a gentle knot near the bud of a second flower.

2. Make the chain longer by continuing to tie flowers together—always making sure to tie the knots as close to the end of the stems as possible, and tighten the knots up near the flower buds.

3. When you're happy with the number of daisies you've linked in your chain, tie the last stem to the flower you began with to make a circle. You can make them in a million sizes—try looping a chain around your neck as a loose-fitting necklace, or try tying a few smaller chains around your wrist for some daisy bracelets!

Make a Killer Scrapbook!

What You'll Need:

* ❊ A HARD-COVER SCRAPBOOK WITH BLANK PHOTO-SAFE PAGES
* ❊ COLORED, PATTERNED, AND TEXTURED PAPER
  (COOL PAPER BRINGS BLANK PAGES TO LIFE. CUT PICTURES IN DIFFERENT-SIZED CIRCLES AND ADHERE TO POLKA DOT PAPER—CUTE! MAKE PAPER POCKETS FOR LOOSE ITEMS.)
* ❊ PHOTO-SAFE STICKY TABS
  (FOR STICKING PICS TO BACKGROUND PAPER AND FOR ADHERING TO PAGES.)
* ❊ FINE-POINT PENS
  (TO IDENTIFY THE WHO, WHAT, WHEN, AND WHERE OF PHOTOS AND KEEPSAKES.)
* ❊ PHOTO-SAFE STICKERS
* ❊ DECORATIVE RULERS
  (FOR CREATING UNIQUE BORDERS LIKE OCEAN WAVES.)

Does it look like Niagara Falls when you open your dresser drawer? Do you have piles of unorganized pics? Don't throw out that sentimental stuff or shove it in a shoebox. Instead, preserve the good times in a totally cool memory book you'll treasure forever.

Put your heart and soul into the album. Find that A+ paper from English and place it in a plastic pocket. Or make a section for your fave poems and song lyrics. Don't leave out special letters from your buds! Oh, and don't forget to leave room for future memories!

Step 1: Hunt and gather

Find some confetti from your last pep rally, a first-place ribbon from swim team, and the best pictures from spring break. Organize the goodies into theme piles. For example, put everything together from one grade or season. Often, you'll need two or three pages for each theme.

Step 2: Keep 'em separated

Toss the junk and separate things that you want to keep in piles that will:

* ✿ go into a handmade paper pocket
* ✿ go into a photo album page
* ✿ be glued onto photo-safe colored paper

Step 3: Bring it all together

Say you want to remember your 12th birthday forever. Had an ice-skating party? There's your theme. Grab the best pics, an invitation, leftover wrapping paper, the guest list, and some skating stickers. Cut a couple of pics into the shape of an ice skate and place them on light blue paper—cut like an ice rink. Focus everything around your theme. Use cutouts (even cookie cutters can be traced to make cool shapes) to make your page pop. Use your imagination—glue a photo from the spring musical right next to a pocket that's holding that rockin' review you clipped from the school newspaper. Do you still have a blankey or pillow from when you were a baby? Cut a piece into a heart shape and place it inside a pocket.

Step 4: Cover it

The outside of your book can display a theme, too. Use markers, buttons, glitter, or whatever fits your personality. Dig animals? Create a jungle theme with zebra stripes, some paper leaves, and bamboo. Or leave the cover blank for a classic book look.

Make a Collage

What You'll Need:
- ❊ A STACK OF OLD *GLs*, OR FAVE PHOTOS
- ❊ GLUE
- ❊ POSTER BOARD
- ❊ SCISSORS

Collages are a really cool way to be creative. If you haven't made one before, here's the skinny:

✿ Think up a theme for your collage—make sure it's something that you really dig, like funky shoes or out-there hairstyles (magazines are good sources for that kind of stuff). If you're using photos, your theme could be the past year in snapshots, including family, friends, your birthday bash, your summer vacation, winter fun, and school highlights.

✿ Group mag pics or snapshots together, according to your theme.

✿ Cut your pics or photos into interesting shapes.

✿ Arrange the collage pieces artistically upon your poster board. There's no right or wrong way to do this—place 'em sideways, upside down, or overlapping each other! Whatever floats your boat.

✿ Glue the pictures onto your poster board as you go, until you've covered every square inch of the board.

✿ Hang your collage on your wall, or use it as a desk topper.

Create a Sidewalk Mural

Just for Fun

When you were little, you spent hours drawing hopscotch games on the sidewalk in front of your house, right? And perhaps you played and wrote your name across the cement in huge, colorful letters? If so, who says you have to stop marking up the streets just 'cause you're growing up? *No one!* So grab your trusty sidewalk chalk and get to work creating a big, beautiful mural! Draw a sunset, a family portrait, whatever strikes your fancy. Have your friends join in and contribute their artistic talents. When you're finished, take a picture of your masterpiece, then say, "So long!" before the next rain washes everything away.

Make a Paper Rose

What You'll Need:

* ❋ SCISSORS
* ❋ TISSUE PAPER (ANY COLOR)
* ❋ RULER
* ❋ GREEN PIPE CLEANERS
* ❋ TAPE
* ❋ GREEN CONSTRUCTION PAPER
* ❋ GLUE

Make yourself (or someone else) a no-maintenance bouquet! One that never needs to be watered, and will never wilt. Tissue paper roses are simple and beautiful, and can be admired anytime, all the time!

1. Cut out a piece of tissue paper measuring 3" x 9". Lay it out flat in front of you so the 3-inch sides are horizontal (on the top and bottom).

2. Starting at the left, fold 1/3 of the tissue paper lengthwise. The paper should now measure 2" x 9".

3. Next, take a green pipe cleaner, and cut it to a length of your choice (this is going to be the stem). Then, tape it to the end of the tissue paper closest to you.

4. To make the bud of your flower, gently and loosely roll the tissue paper around the pipe cleaner. Then pinch the bottom of the tissue paper together, so it's tight against the end of the pipe cleaner.

5. Tape the gathered tissue paper around the pipe cleaner.

6. Cut out a piece of green construction paper that's just big enough to cover the tape, and long enough to wrap around the pipe cleaner twice. Glue it on, over the tape, at the base of the tissue paper bud.

> **HINT:** To make buds of different sizes, experiment with the measurements of your tissue paper. And consider cutting leaf shapes out of extra construction paper, then gluing them onto the pipe cleaner to spruce things up a bit!

Dare to Découpage

What You'll Need:

* ❋ SOMETHING TO DÉCOUPAGE! (PICTURE FRAME, JEWELRY BOX, ANYTHING!)
* ❋ MAGAZINES, MATERIAL AND SCISSORS
* ❋ WHITE GLUE (DILUTE WITH SOME WATER)
* ❋ A POPSICLE STICK, PLASTIC KNIFE, WHATEVER YOU CAN FIND WITH A FLAT, SMOOTH EDGE TO SPREAD AND SMOOTH CUTOUTS OR MATERIAL
* ❋ A PAINT BRUSH OR Q-TIP TO APPLY OR SPREAD GLUE (YOU CAN ALSO FIND SUPPLIES SPECIFICALLY MADE FOR DÉCOUPAGE AT YOUR LOCAL CRAFT STORE)

We admit it—découpage can be a little addicting. It's like once you've magically morphed a mundane frame into a magnificent masterpiece, it's tough to resist the urge to découpage everything. Like that plain pink plastic trash can in your bathroom or the mirror in your room with the fake wood frame—definitely découpage material! From frames to stools to lampshades to lunch boxes to hatboxes to desks to dinner plates, you can découpage almost anything you want. With minimal supplies and limited artistic ability, you can découpage your way into becoming a Découpage Diva. If Mom stockpiles her glossy mags month after month, season after season, ask to leaf through them and thin them out a bit. Or, surely you've saved ALL your *GL* magazines. And if you're willing to cut into them (gulp!), they'll do the trick, too.

Here's How:

1. Ready your clean, dust-free item-to-be-découpaged.

2. Pour over magazines, catalogs, picture books or greeting cards, fabric remnants or wrapping paper to gather collage-worthy pictures, words, or whatever! Stick to a theme: Cats and kittens, tennis, celebrity crushes, trendy fashion, black and white pics— or anything that screams *you*! Consider the size of what you plan to découpage so your cutouts will fit. Think about what you'll be using it for (memory album, birthday present, picture frame). Take into account where it might be used—like if you're making a mirror for your room, make it match your décor!

3. Arrange your cutouts on your object before gluing them—there's nothing worse than trying to move around paper that's soggy with glue goo! Trim and rearrange as necessary for a perfect fit. Of course, your images can overlap and wrap around and stuff.

4. Spread a thin layer of glue where you want to stick your pic and cover the back of the image with glue. Glue it in place. Press your finger down in the center of the cutout and slowly, carefully smooth it down. Flatten any wrinkles as you go. Use your flat spreading thingy if necessary.

5. Continue the process until every image is glued in place.

6. Cover the item with diluted glue (3 parts glue and 1 part water). Let it dry completely.

7. Once dry, coat with several more layers of diluted glue until all edges and corners are totally flat and securely adhered. *Voilà!*

Make Your Own Pet Rock

What You'll Need:
* ❊ THE ROCK OF YOUR CHOICE
* ❊ SHARPIES, MAGIC MARKERS, OR ACRYLIC PAINT

Back in ancient times—the 1970s—a curious fad gripped America. For some WEIRD reason, people raced to adopt pet rocks. That's right—round, little, gray stone buddies. You could actually buy pet rocks at the mall—some came complete with leashes. Maybe there was something in the water, or maybe folks were simply craving a low-maintenance companion that didn't bark all the time or destroy the furniture on a regular basis.

So OK, admit it—pet rocks actually sound just a *little* bit cool. Want to make one yourself? It couldn't be easier. Head outside, and find yourself a rock. Don't worry about choosing a specific size or type—when you set eyes on the rock that's right for you, you'll know it. It's fate!

Bring your rock indoors, and draw a happy little face on it. Give it hair, eyebrows, dimples, whatever. You could also paint your little buddy—multicolor him or her, or paint a funny saying on it. And give your rock a name!

Make sure your rock has a comfy place to dwell—on your desk, your bookshelf, your windowsill, or wherever else you like. Talk with your new little buddy whenever you feel like it. Isn't friendship a beautiful thing?

Make a Shadow Box

What You'll Need:

* ❊ A FAVE PHOTO
* ❊ A CLEAN, EMPTY CEREAL BOX
* ❊ PENCIL
* ❊ SCISSORS
* ❊ COLORED OR WRAPPING PAPER
* ❊ TAPE
* ❊ DECORATIVE STUFF LIKE BOWS, STREAMERS, OR RIBBONS

Want to top your dresser with a really unique picture frame? Try making a shadow box. The effect is pretty cool. You can also use a shadow box to frame your fave figurines, dolls, or other collectibles, too.

Here's the Scoop:

1. Center your picture on the front of the cereal box, trace its outline, and then cut out the shape you traced. (This will make a window in your box.)

2. Cut a piece of colored or wrapping paper that is the exact size of the inside of the cereal box and tape it in place.

3. Place a photo inside the box. Line up the photo with the window, so when you look inside the box, you see it. (Anchor the picture to the back of the box with a little tape.)

4. Decorate the outside of the box any way you like—cover it with cool colored paper and draw or write on it, add bows, streamers, ribbons, whatever!

Funky Book Covers

What You'll Need:

* ❊ **HEAVY-DUTY PAPER** (BROWN GROCERY BAGS, COLORED SHOPPING BAGS FROM YOUR FAVORITE STORE, MEDIUM-WEIGHT WHITE OR COLORED PAPER)
* ❊ **SCISSORS**
* ❊ **HARDBACK BOOK(S) TO COVER**
* ❊ **RULER**
* ❊ **PENCIL**
* ❊ **TAPE**
* ❊ **STICKERS**
* ❊ **MAGAZINES YOU'VE ALREADY READ**
* ❊ **MARKERS** (SHARPIES IN A VARIETY OF COLORS AND SIZES ARE GREAT BECAUSE THEY WORK WELL ON HEAVY PAPER AND WON'T RUN OR FADE)
* ❊ **GLUE**

You've always hit the halls in style. So why should your textbooks be blah? Give them instant personality with DIY book covers!

1. Lay out your paper on a flat, solid surface, like the kitchen table. If you're using paper bags, cut along all seams until you have one large piece of paper.

2. Place your book in the center of the paper, and open it so that the front and back covers are flat against it.

3. Using a ruler, measure out and pencil-mark an excess of about 4- to 5-inches on all sides of your book. Trim it out with scissors.

4. Using your pencil, trace around your actual opened book onto what you just cut out—so you have a rectangle inside a rectangle. Set the book aside.

5. Fold all sides of your paper at the lines you traced around your book. The paper is now the size of your opened book.

6. Insert the front and back bindings of the book's edges into the two side (vertical) folds. To secure, you can use pieces of tape on the cover, but don't tape the book!

7. Your book is comfortably snuggled into its new cover? Good. Kick up the creativity—put those stickers, magazine cutouts, and markers to good use.

Chapter 10

Beautify Your Room

Time to roll up your sleeves and give your crib a makeover! A little rearranging here, a few pretty accents there, a tad of neat 'n' tidy— and *voilà*! An almost-like-new boudoir. Hey, it's *your* space, so why not make it special?

Closet Makeover!

What You'll Need:

❈ A CAMERA (POLARIOD, DIGITAL, OR ANY KIND THAT YOU HAVE)

❈ TAPE

❈ SHOE BOXES

❈ A PAD AND PEN

Say so long to insanely hectic you're-still-in-your-closet-searching-for-just-the-right-black-turtleneck-to-go-with-your-mini-pleated-skirt-as-the-bus-pulls-away-from-the-curb mornings forever! Spend an afternoon organizing complete school outfits in advance, and you'll be able to sport a full fashion look Monday morn with time to spare.

Here are the How-Tos:

❀ Make up ten fab, complete outfits. Include the right socks or tights, shoes, bag, and jewelry to match each look.

❀ Pull one complete outfit out of your closet. Lay it out on your bed.

❀ Point your camera at the outfit and snap a pic.

❀ When your photos are developed, tack them on a bulletin board inside your closet.

❀ Re-hang outfit number one in your closet, grouping together each piece of every ensemble for easy grabbin'.

❀ Pull out your next outfit. Repeat the instructions above.

❀ While you're at it, organize your shoes by snapping a picture of each pair, putting the pair into a box, and taping the developed photo to the box side that faces out. Then stack the shoe boxes neatly on your closet floor.

❀ Might as well take inventory of your socks and undies, too. Examine each pair in your drawers for rips, holes, and wear and tear. Toss out what's hopeless, and make a list of the stuff you need to replace on your next shopping trip!

Stash Your Barbies

What You'll Need:
* ❋ YOUR BARBIE INVENTORY
* ❋ TISSUE PAPER
* ❋ SMALL PLASTIC CLOTHING BAGS WITH ZIPPERS
* ❋ CARDBOARD BOXES
* ❋ PACKING TAPE
* ❋ A BLACK SHARPIE

Old Barbie dolls are among the most valuable collectibles. Did you know that the first Barbie ever made is worth thousands of bucks today? It's true!

Even Barbies from recent years go up in value really quickly. If you've been thinking of booting your Babs from your room, why not store your dolls smart and safe so you can sell them someday if you want to?

Wrap your Barbies individually in tissue paper. Place each one in her own plastic clothing bag, and zip it up. (Important note: If by chance you have any of the original boxes your Barbies came in, store your dolls inside of them—it increases their value.) Place all your Barbies in cardboard boxes, then seal with packing tape. Mark "Fragile-Barbies!" clearly on each box.

You can store Barbie clothes and accessories the same way. If your Barbies happen to have unfortunate haircuts, or are permanently marked up or damaged, you probably won't ever be able to sell them. Nor should you part with your favorites. You and the President-of-the-United States Barbie have been through a lot together, so she's earned her spot on your dresser, and in your heart—for good!

Give Your Room Some Feng Shui

What You'll Need:

❋ A DESIRE FOR POSITIVE ENERGY

Have you ever noticed how some places make you feel anxious and tired while other places make you feel relaxed and full of energy? Did you ever imagine that the things around you—your furniture, books, and even a beanbag chair—could have a powerful effect on you?

Whoa! Welcome to the world of Feng Shui (pronounced "fung shway"). Feng Shui is the Chinese art of arranging furniture and decorations in such a way in order to create positive energy! By designing a room to make you feel and do your best, you're putting the forces of nature on your side. Here's how to Feng Shui, your way.

1. Clutter. In Feng Shui, clutter is the first thing you should tackle. Believe it or not, if there's a mess in any square of your room (see the map), it could have a messy effect on the area of your life that square represents.

If the clutter is in the middle of the left side of your room, for example, in the square that relates to "Family", at-home relationships could become particularly complicated and bothersome. Have you been fighting with your brother or sister a lot lately? Take a look around and see where you can straighten up your room—and your life.

2. Your Bed. Feng Shui experts say that sleeping too close to the door might make you feel tired and spaced out when you wake up in the morning because your door brings in a lot of energy—too much, in fact, to be able to have a good night's sleep.

The best place to put your bed is as far from the door as possible, which would be in the corner diagonal from your door. If your door is in the middle of the wall, your bed can be in either corner across from it. Another reason to put your bed across the room is because the two corners opposite your door—the squares that represent "Wealth & Prosperity" and "Relationships"—are powerful spots, and sleeping there could make you feel more confident and energized when you wake up in the morning.

If your room is too small and you can't move your bed, you might want to hang a crystal between the bed and the door. That should deflect some of the energy and make you feel more energized when you wake up.

3. Your Desk. Both corners opposite your door have the best energy, so consider putting your desk in a remaining corner. Then, have it face the door.

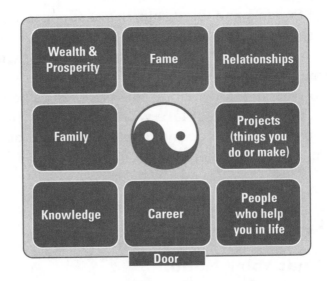

That might seem weird at first, but according to Feng Shui, you shouldn't have your back to the door. If you can't see what's sneaking up on you—like your little sister—it could give you the feeling you don't have control over things in your life.

If you face your door, you may feel more confident in solving problems you're having with schoolwork, friends, or family. If you'd rather have your desk face the wall but also want to increase your confidence, there's a simple solution: You can hang a mirror up on the wall so you can see what's behind you!

4. Your Dresser. Where your dresser goes is not too important. Just be sure not to put it behind your door so closely that the door won't open all the way. This could cut off the flow of energy coming in through the door. The same goes for laundry baskets, stereos, and anything else that might stop the door from opening all the way.

5. Windows. If your windows are positioned directly across from your door in such a way that you can see straight out them the minute you step into your room, a lot of the energy might be escaping from your room. As a result, you might feel bored, spaced-out, or tired. To get reenergized, hang wind chimes or a crystal on a red string between the door and window.

Crystals and wind chimes are supposed to catch the energy and disperse it around the room, making you feel happier, more upbeat, and better able to concentrate. Crystals or wind chimes could also make you feel like you have more control over problems and their solutions. So what are you waiting for? No need to paint or spend tons of money on new décor. Just take what you already have and move it around your room to the appropriate spots. Be sure to get your folks to sign off on your rearrangement first!

Decorate Your Dresser

SOLO

What You'll Need:
  * A DRESSER (AND PERMISSION FROM YOUR FOLKS TO CHANGE IT UP)
  * KNOB ACCENTS (SEE IDEAS BELOW)
  * GLUE

Want to give that old dresser that's hogging space in your room an instant face-lift? Decorate the drawer knobs! You can find beautiful antique-style buttons at the craft store for cheap, and just glue them on top of your existing knobs for a totally new look. Or get puffy pom-poms from the fabric store and glue those on the existing ones instead. Other neat possibilities: Beanie Babies or small doll heads glued onto knobs. Or just paint the knobs a cool color with paint made for whatever material your knobs are made of (ask a grown-up for help with this), so they'll stand out against your dresser's color!

Chapter 11

The Write Stuff

Break out the pen and paper! Nobody expects you to land a Pulitzer (not right off the bat, anyway), but try your hand at turning your words and thoughts into ink. Heck, maybe your teacher will even give you extra credit for your A+ effort.

Speak Your Own Speak

What You'll Need:

❋ A LOVE FOR BUZZWORDS

Ever wonder where new slang words come from? Yeah, movies and songs, sometimes, but someone has to think up all those new def sayings. So, hey, why not you? Brainstorm freestyle with your buds for fresh ways to communicate. A few ideas to get you started:

LINNER—A combination of lunch and dinner. Sample usage: "I had breakfast so late, I wasn't hungry till like five o'clock, so I just grabbed some *linner.*"

TATER TOT (new usage)—What you call your little sister when she won't get out of her jammies and away from the cartoons on Saturday morning. Sample usage: "If that *tater tot* doesn't get off the sofa soon, she's gonna grow up to be a full-blown couch potato."

GLOOMER-DOOMER—Someone who grooves on a negative tip. Sample usage: "I hate being a *gloomer-doomer*. I always see the glass as half-empty, not half-full."

Write Your Own Fortune Cookie Fortunes   Just for Fun

Just finished your pu-pu platters at Peking Gardens? It's fortune cookie time! You grab your cookie and bust it open, psyched to read all about the fame, money, and success that awaits you. Instead, you find this lame little saying: "A stitch in time saves nine." Bummer!

If you don't like the fortune fate has stuffed inside your cookie, make your own luck! Take out a pad of paper, rip it into little strips, pass them out, and have everybody at the table write one new fortune. Now one person should grab all the finished fortunes, plop 'em into a dry, empty tea cup, and shake 'em up. Then everyone gets to pluck out a new and improved fortune, and read it out loud to the table.

Write Fan Letters to Your Friends and Family

What You'll Need:

❋ **A PAD OF PAPER**

You've probably written a fan letter or two in your time, which is way cool. But just for today, let somebody else give your fav celeb her well-deserved props. Turn your attention to your friends and family for a minute!

How cool would it be to write every important person in your life a fan letter detailing all of their good qualities? You can remind them of the wonderful favors they've done for you over time, and let them know how much they mean to you.

Write all of your peeps their own special note, then mail the notes off. Don't give off any clues that the letters are coming. The most wonderful thing about receiving a fan letter is the element of happy surprise. Your buds and family just might shower you right back with compliments in no time—not that that's the reason you should write fan letters in the first place. Still, one good deed deserves another—maybe you'll get a few fan letters of your own!

Do You Haiku?

What You'll Need:
* A PAD OF PAPER
* A PENCIL

Love to write poetry? Expand your skills by giving haiku a shot. Haiku is an ancient form of Japanese verse that's really fun and easy to create—it's just three lines. You don't rhyme words in haiku, but you do follow this form:

✿ Five syllables in the first line

✿ Seven syllables in the second line

✿ Five syllables in the third line

✿ Nature is a really popular topic in the world of haiku— think about the wind, sky, woods, beach, insects, animals, or birds. Here's an example:

> *Red feathered robin*
> *Flies onto my windowsill*
> *Singing "Good morning!"*

It's as easy as that! The more haiku you write, the better feeling you'll have for its style and rhythm. So grab your pen and get going!

Letter to the Editor

What You'll Need:
* EMAIL OR STATIONERY
* YOUR FAVORITE (OR LEAST FAVORITE) MAGAZINE
* AN OPINION

Have you ever written a letter to the editor to express your opinion about a story? Whether you really loved something, or were totally offended by an article, editors love to know your opinions. That's how they know what you're digging and what you're not. These tips will not only get your letter read, but possibly published!

When you have a complaint: You bought a magazine and it seemed to have only boy advice, makeup tips, and expensive everything. Tell the editor how you feel, but do it smart, and with direction. Exactly which stories reinforced this girls-are-cheesy theory? Find them, and cite the titles. Clearly state your point in the first sentence: "Your story 'How to Snag Your Crush' was offensive to me because it makes it seem like all boys are idiots and all girls are boy-hunting desperados!" Then state why you like the mag, but wish they would include more important feature stories, like true stories about real girls.

When you love a story: Editors simply love it when you pay them compliments. But in order not to be too self-congratulatory, they usually print the letters that talk directly about the magazine and what was in a recent month. Be specific: State the article title and why you liked it, reinforcing that this mag ALWAYS remembers that girls are thinkers (or whatever your point is). That's the kind of letter that makes it in. Trust us!

Message in a Bottle — Just for (Summer) Fun

Liven up your next trip to the seashore! Write a message, stuff it into a sealable bottle (make sure your message stays dry; seal the bottle tightly with a cap or a cork), and drop it into the ocean. It's also an awesome way to try to find out about new people and new places. How amazing would it be if someone across the ocean wrote back to you and told you all about herself and where she lives?

In your message, mention a little bit about yourself, your hometown, and the ocean area or beach where you sent off the message. Ask whoever reads your message to fill in about the same type of stuff on their end—include a mailing address where they can write back to you. Then toss your bottle into the ocean, and see what happens!

Master Calligraphy

What You'll Need:

 ❋ A PILE OF 8-1/2" X 11" PAPER (LINED)

 ❋ A CALLIGRAPHY PEN (THERE ARE TWO DIFFERENT OPTIONS.
   A CALLIGRAPHY SET IS A LITTLE MORE EXPENSIVE—USUALLY STARTING
   AT AROUND $15—AND ALLOWS YOU TO CHANGE PEN TIPS. YOU'LL ALSO
   NEED TO HAVE SOME BLACK INDIA INK TO WRITE WITH—THAT USUALLY
   RUNS ABOUT $5 A BOTTLE. OR, YOU CAN ALWAYS PICK UP JUST A
   CALLIGRAPHY PEN THAT IS MORE LIKE A MARKER—AVAILABLE FOR
   ABOUT $1 TO $2 AT STATIONERY, ART, OR OFFICE SUPPLY STORES.)

Calligraphy is a beautiful, swirly, fancy style of penmanship that
looks cool on invitations and handwritten letters. It's really fun
to teach yourself, too, by copying the letters. Here are some
basic tips to get you started:

 ✿ A calligraphy pen has a specially slanted tip, and is the key
   to creating lovely letters. Hold the calligraphy pen as you
   would a regular pen or pencil. (Try to keep the tip of your pen
   slanted at a 45-degree angle when you touch it to the paper.)

 ✿ Carefully look at the example calligraphy alphabet below, and
   start to copy the letters. You can start drawing the letters from
   anywhere—although it's generally easiest if you start drawing

Aa Bb Cc Dd Ee Ff Gg

Hh Ii Jj Kk Ll Mm

Nn Oo Pp Qq Rr Ss Tt

Uu Vv Ww Xx Yy Zz

from the top. If you want, place some paper over the alphabet below and try tracing the letters onto your paper first, to get a better feel for how and where the letters swirl.

❀ Keep practicing—the more you work at calligraphy, the prettier your handwriting will get. Once you feel comfortable with drawing each letter in alphabetical order, try mixing them up and before you know it you'll be writing someone a fancy letter!

Write Your Life Story

What You'll Need:
❈ **A PAD OF PAPER OR A JOURNAL**
❈ **THE WRITING UTENSIL OF YOUR CHOICE**

Yes, most people are a little bit older when they sit down to write about their lives. But your life story so far has plenty of fascinating elements for sure—so why wait to put them down on paper? You've accomplished tons already!

Think about it. You've felt happiness and sadness—as everyone has. You've enjoyed fabulous, fun experiences. You've learned tons of stuff— in school, from your family, from dealing with your friends (and maybe a few enemies). Your life so far has been way interesting!

Describe the highlights of your life to the present day. An easy way to do this is to write about the most important stuff that's happened to you, the good and the bad, as if you were telling your story to a complete stranger. If a person didn't know you from a hole in the wall, yet you had to get the key stuff about yourself across to him or her, you'd be forced to recognize which events in your life were really a major deal, and which events were less important.

Write as little or as much as you'd like. Read over the story to yourself when you're done. It can help you feel really good about how far you've come—about the probs you've solved, and about what a cool person you are!

Chapter 12

Get Sporty

Why are you just laying there? There's a great, big, beautiful world around you, so get out and appreciate it! There are tons of games and activities you can do in your own backyard—weather permitting, of course. But, on the right day, you can play, play, play.

Learn to Juggle

What You'll Need:

* THREE LIGHTWEIGHT RAQUETBALLS, VELCRO BALLS, OR OTHER SMALL, SOFT BALLS
* GOOD HAND-EYE COORDINATION

Juggling is tons of fun, not to mention a real lifesaver during rough baby-sitting gigs. Here are some easy tips to help you give it a try:

* Start by simply tossing one ball in the air, back and forth between your hands. If you're right-handed, toss from your right hand; if you're a lefty, shoot from your left. Keep your eye focused on the motion of the ball.

* Slowly begin to toss the ball a little higher. Move your hands apart a bit wider, too.

* When you're comfy with the rhythm of one moving ball, pick up a second one. Toss it into the air after the first ball from the opposite hand. Keeping your focus now on the second ball, try to keep both balls moving in the air at once. This takes time to master.

* To add the third ball, use your bud as a spotter. Once you get used to the rhythm of two balls moving from your hands through the air and back again, take an eye off that motion, and focus on your spotter. When you feel comfortable, give her a nod. Your spotter should toss in the third ball, toward your right-hand side.

NOTE: Expect to make tons of mistakes at first. The third ball is advanced stuff, but you can do it!

Hit the Park and Fly a Kite

WITH A GROUP OF BUDS

What You'll Need:

- ✻ **4 PIECES OF THIN PAPER (LIKE NEWSPAPER), EACH 11-1/2" x 19"**
- ✻ **A RULER**
- ✻ **TAPE**
- ✻ **SCISSORS**
- ✻ **LOTS OF STURDY STRING**
- ✻ **HOLE PUNCH** (OPTIONAL)

There's nothing more exciting and exhilarating than the feeling you get when you're running across the grass with the wind against your back, holding a flapping kite aloft in the spring breeze. If you and your crew haven't tried kite flying, you don't know what you're missing!

You can find kites at department, hobby, toy, and sporting goods stores for only a few dollars each. Paper kites fly best in light, gentle breezes. Plastic or cloth kites can handle wind that's a little stronger. The only time you really shouldn't fly a kite is when it's majorly gusty outside. A harsh breeze can wreck your kite in two seconds flat. When flying your kite, limit your airspace to areas that are free of trees, electrical wires, telephone poles, low buildings, and walls. A clear, open area means clear, open sailing—and hours of fun! But, you don't have to buy a kite! You can always make your own:

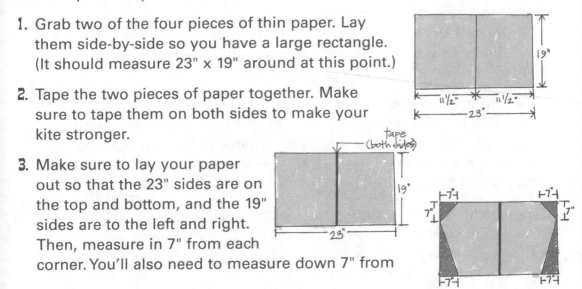

1. Grab two of the four pieces of thin paper. Lay them side-by-side so you have a large rectangle. (It should measure 23" x 19" around at this point.)

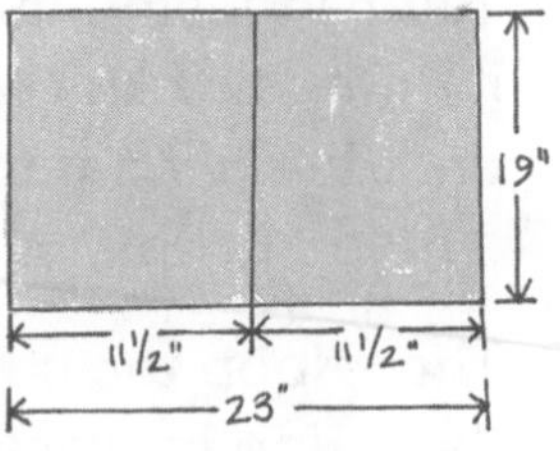

2. Tape the two pieces of paper together. Make sure to tape them on both sides to make your kite stronger.

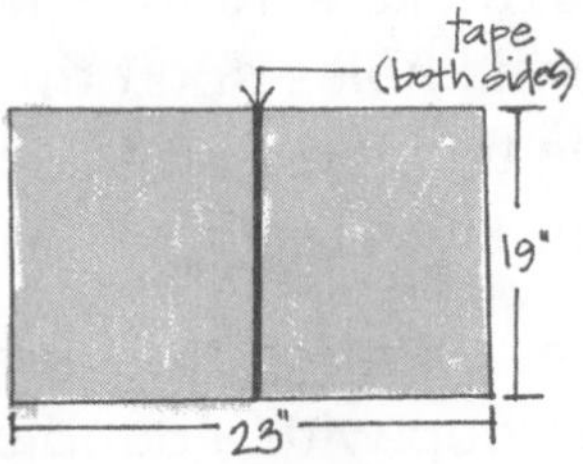

3. Make sure to lay your paper out so that the 23" sides are on the top and bottom, and the 19" sides are to the left and right. Then, measure in 7" from each corner. You'll also need to measure down 7" from

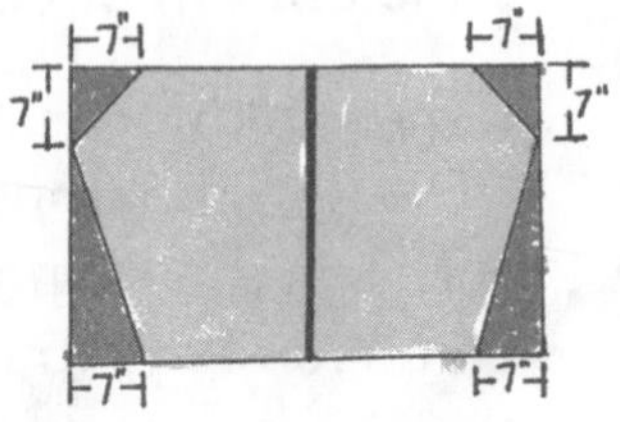

the top corner. Draw diagonal lines to connect each
point (as shown).

4. Cut along the lines to give
your kite its shape.

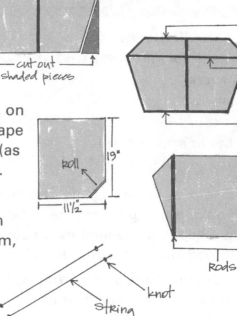

cut out —
shaded pieces

tape all sides

5. Tape around all edges of your kite, on
both sides of the paper. Also use tape
to connect the points of your kite, (as
shown). Do this on both sides, too.

roll

19"

11½"

6. Take the remaining two pieces
of 11-1/2" x 19" paper and roll them
diagonally (the tighter you roll them,
the better your kite will hold up).
When you're finished rolling each
paper, you should have two long,
sturdy, sticklike rods that are the
same height as your kite. Attach
them with tape, (as shown).

Rods

knot

string

7. Cut two pieces of string, each measuring
5' long. Tie a knot at both ends.

8. Secure the string to your kite (as shown).
You can fasten the string either by taping
it onto your kite (on the side opposite the rods), or by tying it
on. (If you want to tie the string to your kite, you'll need to use
a hole punch and punch holes in your kite.)

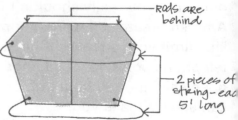

Rods are
behind

2 pieces of
string—eac
5' long

9. Then, loop the string through the hole and tie a double-knot to keep
the string in place. Make sure to reinforce around the holes with
plenty of tape, so the holes don't rip when you fly your kite! You
should have made two loops, one near the top, and one at
the bottom of your kite.

double
knot

10. Cut one more piece of string that is 15' long.
Tie it to the upper loop with a double knot.
This is the string you'll be holding when
you're ready to take on the wind!

15' of
string—
to
hola

Work It Out!

What You'll Need:

⁎ A PEDOMETER (UNDER $10 AT ANY SPORTING GOODS OR DEPARTMENT STORE)

⁎ A DESIRE TO GET IN SHAPE WITHOUT HAVING TO COMMIT TO WORKING OUT

You'd rather eat worms than work out? We have an easy solution. Experts say that walking for a few miles a day is a great way to get healthy. And you might already be walking more than you think. A really fun way to track exactly how far your little legs carry you in an average day is to don a pedometer. Pedometers are like little stopwatch devices. You can clip one to your belt or wear it around a wrist or ankle. As you walk to school, through the halls between classes, around the house— your pedometer will calculate your movements in miles. At the end of the day, check how many miles' worth of walking you completed. Log over two miles and know that you are helping yourself stay fit!

Go Bowling...At Home!

What You'll Need:

⁎ 10 EMPTY 1-LITER SODA BOTTLES

⁎ A BALL (LIKE A TENNIS BALL)

There's no such thing as a gutterball when you go bowling at home! And it's fun to play either inside or outside. All you have to do is fill ten soda bottles with a little bit of water (just enough so they don't blow over—you can add a little sand to the inside if the bottles seem kind of wobbly), and set them up like they do at bowling lanes. Make four rows of bottles, placing one in the first row, stagger two in the second, three in the third, and the remaining four in the last row. You should end up with a triangular set-up. Then, grab the ball and start bowling!

Take turns bowling with your friends. Each person should get two chances to roll the ball per turn. If you want to keep score (but you definitely don't have to), keep track of the number of "pins" each person knocks down per turn. Decide with your friends on how many times you want to bowl—there isn't any set amount of turns you have to take.

This is your game, so it can end whenever you and your friends desire. When you're finished, total up the score. Whoever took down the most pins is the winner. So, what are you waiting for? Strike it up!

Back Yard Mini-Golf

What You'll Need:

* ✳ PAPER CUPS
* ✳ PAPER PLATES
* ✳ SMALL WOODEN BOARDS
* ✳ FOR A CLUB: BROOM, MOP, OR A STICK WILL DO
* ✳ FOR A BALL: ANY SMALL BALL THAT WILL FIT INTO THE CUP, LIKE A TENNIS BALL, PINGPONG BALL, OR GOLF BALL

Channel your inner Tiger Woods by setting up a golf course on your very own turf this Spring. It's easy!

Here's How:

1. Remember that a golf course normally has eighteen holes. If your yard space is tight and you have to skimp, do twelve holes.

2. DON'T DIG HOLES ALL OVER THE YARD! Use paper cups, secured into the dirt, to make holes. To space your cups correctly, measure out about twelve to eighteen feet between them, depending on the size of your yard. Space the cups closer together at the start of your course, and farther apart toward the end. You can measure the space between the cups easily by walking the course, putting one foot directly in front of the other, toes touching your heel, and counting about one foot out per step you take.

3. You can make little ramps to shoot through by using pieces of wood propped up on rocks (make sure the rocks are high enough so that there's a space under the board to shoot through), or heavyweight paper plates folded in half with edges jammed down into the dirt. The easiest way to do this is by setting your wood or plate on a slant, like wherever there's a little hill or bump in your yard.

4. When you're ready to play, keep the number of players using your course to a maximum of four at a time (two or three is actually ideal). Otherwise, conditions will get way too cramped in such a small space.

5. The special rules of backyard mini-golf: Starting at the first hole, players take turns trying to tap their ball into the cup, using a broom, mop or stick as your club, unless you have actual golf clubs, of course. You want to get your ball into each cup in the least number of shots. Give each player one point for each shot it takes to get her ball into each cup— whoever has the lowest score at the end of the course wins!

HINT: Don't get carried away and whack that ball too hard, or it might just sail right over your fence and through your neighbor's picture window. The 'rents would NOT be pleased. Play it safe by using your backyard course not to perfect your swing, but instead, to perfect your stroke technique.

Walk This Way!

WITH A GROUP OF BUDS

What You'll Need:
* ❋ **WORKOUT CLOTHES**
* ❋ **SNEAKS**

Take part in a walkathon for charity! Not only is it great exercise, but there are few better uses of your free time than using it to raise money to help others. Sign up a ton of sponsors, then walk with your buds. You'll meet lots of neat new people, too.

Take a Tumble into a Big Pile of Leaves   Just for Fun

Falling into a huge, crunchy pile of leaves has got to be one of Autumn's most groovy pleasures. Don't deny yourself!

Broom Hockey

WITH A GROUP OF BUDS

What You'll Need:

- **ONE BROOM PER PLAYER**
- **ONE TENNIS BALL**
- **SOMETHING TO SERVE AS GOALMARKERS AND A CENTERLINE** (TRY RUMMAGING AROUND IN YOUR GARAGE FOR STUFF THAT'S SUITABLE)

Who said brooms only come in handy for witches and chores? It's a little known fact that they're also great to use as sports equipment—like as baseball bats and hockey sticks. Seriously. So dig around in the storage closet at home and nab the broom (after making sure it's OK with your folks, of course). Then round up your buds for a great game of broom hockey.

Lots of people think hockey can only be played on ice, but that isn't true. Broom hockey can be played anywhere, during any season. It's just as fun to play the game in the snow or grass as it is to play on ice. (If you do play broom hockey on ice, be careful and make sure that the ice is thick enough to be tromping on!)

Before you start playing, you'll want to divide the group into two teams. Then decide on some rules—about boundaries, possession, how long you're going to play, and stuff that might get tricky during the game if you don't go over it first—and make sure that everyone knows and understands them. Consider the area around where you're playing and figure out how big you want your "rink" to be. Then designate an area at each end and make those the team goals. (This is where the stuff from your garage comes in handy. Make sure to leave plenty of space for your goal so you can swat the tennis ball at an angle and still make it in...but don't make the area too big, or you'll never be able to defend it!) The last thing you do before starting to play is to indicate the centerline, because you have to start your game from there!

To start the game, pick one person from each team to go to the centerline for a face-off. Place the tennis ball between the two people facing off, then have someone count to three and shout, "Go!" Whoever smacks the tennis ball first gets control of the game, and that person can pass the ball to her teammates, as long as no one touches it with their hands. If someone on the team with control *does* touch the ball with their hands, that team has to give up possession, and the ball transfers to the other side. Possession also switches from one team to the other when someone scores—for example, if Team A scores a goal, Team B automatically gets possession of the ball.

Once you're playing, broom hockey is more or less about going back and forth and trying to score the most goals. It's real easy to play—you just need to get out there and have fun!

Recreate the Beach on the Roof of Your Apartment Building

Just for (Summer) Fun

What You'll Need:

* PORTABLE RADIO/CD PLAYER
* WADING POOL
* BEACH TOWELS
* SUNSCREEN
* PORTABLE FAN, BATTERY OPERATED

You can make your own beach on the roof of your apartment building (but keep in mind, we're only suggesting this IF you have permissible rooftop access). So, slip on your flip flops, and head for the stairs. This also works in any backyard, too! Your beach set-up: You and your buds can spread out towels and beach chairs just as you would at the ocean. Your portable fan is a good stand-in for a sea breeze. Crank up your radio just as you would at the shore, playing lots of summer mood music (like "Soak Up the Sun" by Sheryl Crow). Fill a baby pool with water using buckets of water toted out from your bathtub, or from a garden hose, and dip your toes in to your heart's delight. The only beachy element missing? Sand! But do you really miss the way it collects inside the folds of your swimsuit and in between your toes? Doubt it!

Be a Ball Girl

What You'll Need:

* ❄ SPEEDY SNEAKS
* ❄ AN EAGLE EYE
* ❄ SPRINTING ABILITY

Love tennis? Why not volunteer to work as a ball girl at your local tennis club this summer? If you've ever watched Wimbledon or the U.S. Open on TV, you know the drill: Ball girls (and boys) stand at the back of the court and kneel on either side of the net during matches. When someone hits a ball out of bounds or dumps one into the net, the ball girls run and scoop them up.

If you want to learn to be a ball girl, you'll need to be fast on your feet, have good hand/eye coordination and love (and understand) tennis. Who knows, you might work your way up to the U.S. Open before long!

Build a Snow Family

Just for (Winter) Fun

What You'll Need:

* ❄ SNOW CLOTHES
* ❄ KILLER SNOW GLOVES
* ❄ WARM HAT
* ❄ SNOW PEOPLE ACCESSORIES FROM THE KITCHEN
* ❄ A STEREO

Why build a snowman when you can build a snow family? Doesn't the idea of making a snowgirl sound fun? Everyone is always building snowmen! Enough—time to give female and kid snowpeople equal play. Start by grabbing the accessories you'll need to create noses, eyes, and any clothes, hats, or other stuff you'll want to dress your icy family in. Hey, you could make YOURSELVES, too! Make whomever or whatever (a snowdog?) you want, and if it's a snowman, then OK. But *please* don't forget to at least make him a girlfriend. Snowmen get lonely, too.

Chapter 13

Fun with the Fam

There's no one around to hang with except your mom? Or sib? Or dad? So what? Bonding with kinfolk can be fun! But for a change of pace, put away the Monopoly or Yahtzee for now. Here are some ideas to really put you in touch with the family bunch.

Go Back In Time: Uncover Your Family History

What You'll Need:

* ❊ CURIOSITY AND FAMILY PRIDE

How'd your grandparents come to America? How did they meet? What was your great Aunt Lydia really like—you know, the great-aunt everybody says you look like? Ask your 'rents and grand-'rents, and any other relatives to give you the scoop on the old days! Hang out, ask questions, take notes, or tape your conversations to preserve your family history for the next generation. Get to know your family, who they are now, who they were before, and who came before them. You'll be glad you did.

Maybe Mom or Grandma have old albums or scrapbooks stashed away in the attic. Dust off your precious family memorabilia and take a trip back in time. Put together the big picture—and while we're talking about pictures, ask if you can frame that photo of Gram when she was your age and put it on your desk. For more info on researching your family or creating a family tree, type your last name into an Internet search engine. Pretty cool to find out how far back your roots might go!

Create a Family Quiz

What You'll Need:

* ❊ PEN AND PAPER
* ❊ THE 411 ON THE FAM

How well does your family know each other? Make up a quiz using key factoids you know about your relatives, and quiz everybody at your next family dinner or reunion. Stick to safe, non-embarrassing info (if you know your 14-year-old cousin Joey still sleeps with the light on from time to time, keep that to yourself, please). And be willing to poke a little good-natured fun at yourself, too—see who in the family can guess you're the one who has had a secret, lifelong fear of beets! (Which is totally understandable, by the way.)

Make Mom an MTV Groupie!

What You'll Need:

* ✳ A BLANK AUDIO TAPE OR A BLANK CD
* ✳ A CD PLAYER/TAPE RECORDER OR A CD BURNER
* ✳ YOUR CD COLLECTION

How many times have you been riding in the car, totally grooving to your favorite Ashanti hit—and your mom was like, "Is that Janet Jackson?" Uh…*noooooo*. You've got to hand it to your Mom for at least TRYING. Believe it or not, Moms like cool music, too! So why not learn about her fave tunes—and clue her in about yours—by trading music? Make Mom her own fun and funky mix tape of the hip sounds you love, from your own CD collection. Ask your brother or sister if they want to put their musical two cents in, too. Now, when choosing tunes, be gentle. Ease Mom into your sounds by keeping the vibe mellow, but the beat funky.

Hand Mom your finished creation, and don't be surprised if you find out she can sing along to every word on it the next time she drives you to b-ball practice!

Bust a Move with Mom

What You'll Need:

* ✳ TO PUSH THE FURNITURE BACK IN THE LIVING ROOM
* ✳ A STEREO
* ✳ YOUR MOM'S OLD RECORD AND TAPE COLLECTIONS

We know, we know—the idea of your mom bustin' a move is kinda funny. Maybe she can really boogie, though—you've never really seen her get down, have you? That's about to change! Clear the living room floor and ask Mom to dig out her favorite prehistoric tunes. Have her show you all the dance steps that were cool when she was your age! You might really dig a few of her old-school dances—and once you've learned them, you can teach them to your buds!

Call a Long-lost Relative

What You'll Need:
* A TELEPHONE

Your cousin Wendi was constantly by your side when you were little. Things change, though. Wendi's dad got transferred out of state three years ago. Even though you promised to call and write each other every week, gradually you and Wendi lost touch. It's not that you stopped wanting to talk to her, it's just that you got way busy with cheering after school, and you made some new friends—there just doesn't seem to be enough time in your life to keep in touch.

Make some! It's important to talk to a cool cousin like Wendi whenever you can manage it. When you form a real bond with somebody in life, it's key to realize how rare and awesome it is. Of course, you shouldn't expect to share the same day-to-day closeness with Wendi you had when she lived nearby. That's OK though, because a strong sense of family and friendship can survive separations. You guys might have even cooler stuff to talk about, now that you've each had new experiences.

Pick up the phone and give your cuz a buzz. You might feel a little awkward and nervous at first—but she'll surely be psyched to hear from you. Don't freak over what to talk about with her, either. The best way to break the ice: Ask Wendi what SHE'S been up to first. She's probably got tons of exciting stories to tell you—and will definitely want to know what's been up with you as well.

The bottom line: You can reconnect with a long-lost relative, no matter how much time has passed. Just don't let any more time go by without saying hi!

Create a Family Newsletter: You're the Editor!

What You'll Need:

❋ A DESIRE TO CATCH UP WITH YOUR RELATIVES

EXTRA! EXTRA! Read all about it! If you have a super-gigantic extended family, this is a great way to keep in touch and to keep up with busy lives! Email or call relatives to find out who's psyched to contribute to the newsletter. Then send a mass message to all your contributors, giving them the rundown. Your newsletter needs a title. You need to decide how often you plan to publish. How are you going to organize it? A section for each immediate family group or by topics like school, work, sports, etc. If you're not sure what works best for your family, pose these options to contributors and go ahead with the majority vote.

Give family members a deadline to send you their news. Then, it will be up to you to organize it, add your own news and then distribute it via email or snail mail! If you can include pictures and drawings, that's even better!

See Ya!

Phew! You've done every craft, every activity, and have had every ounce of fun you're gonna have? Wrong! Now that you've done all of the boredom busters in this book, it's time to tell us your favorite ways to have fun! Have a super-cool craft you and your buds love to make? Know a yummy snack recipe? Share with us your majorly inventive activities and extra-entertaining ideas—we'd love to know! Either hop onto a computer and check out this month's website where you can post your ideas online, or send your thoughts to us at:

Boredom Buster Ideas!
GL
4517 Harford Road
Baltimore, MD. 21214

You never know—your boredom buster could appear in our next issue of *GL* magazine or be featured on the club website!

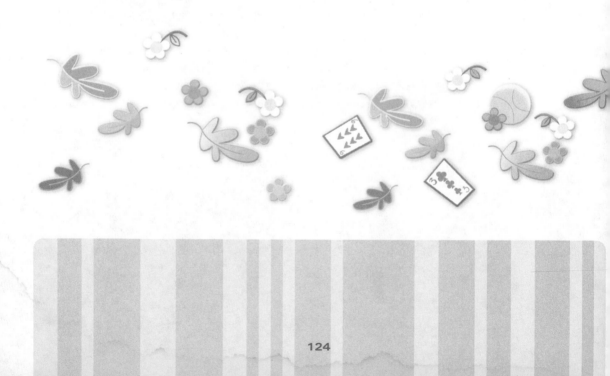